Longman

'O' Level English

Power-Packed

Vocabulary

Ho Lin Lee & Irene Yeow

PEARSON
Longman

Thematic Framework • Challenging • Empowering

Pearson Education South Asia Pte Ltd
23/25 First Lok Yang Road, Singapore 629733

Associated companies, branches and representatives throughout
the world

First published 2007
Third reprint 2009

ISBN   978-981-06-0734-0
ISBN-10   981-06-0734-2

Produced by Pearson Education South Asia Pte Ltd
Printed in Singapore

The
publisher's
policy is to use
paper manufactured
from sustainable forests

Preface

Vocabulary building is often nobody's idea of fun. Therefore, we have conceptualised this book by incorporating fun and enjoyable elements into the expansion of your vocabulary. As you leaf through this book, you will notice that it's different from most vocabulary books. Not only does this book enhance your vocabulary, it also equips you with the necessary skills needed to familiarise you with common and not-so-common words. Furthermore, myriad word games and activities are incorporated to enhance your memory of word meanings and their usage.

Another significant difference between this book and the standard vocabulary book is that while the latter deals with words in a 'detached' manner, this book is also concerned with the writing aspects: you are encouraged to use word-worthy words in your writing through sentence-making exercises.

The vocabulary words are organised in units of specified themes. A thematic framework has proved to be a helpful and effective aid in learning new words because the unknown words are given a context; association of words with context helps one to recognise and remember the words more easily.

To go a step further, we have organised the material into three parts:

Part 1   **Building Your Vocabulary**
Part 2   **Tackling the Vocabulary Question in the GCE 'O' Level English Language Paper 2**
Part 3   **GCE 'O' Level Words You Should Know**

Part 1 incorporates word games, crossword puzzles, fill-in-the-blank exercises, choose-the-correct-option exercises, sentence making, word search, scrabble-type pursuits and other word activities to help you build your vocabulary in a fun and painless way. For some units, a Vocab List is added at the end of the unit for learning reinforcement. This list includes words tested in the unit together with their meanings.

Part 2 reinforces examination-oriented skills which you can utilise in tackling 'language appreciation' and vocabulary type of questions in the GCE 'O' level English language paper.

Part 3 contains a list of essential words, in alphabetical order, that you should know before you sit for the examination. Instead of giving a mere list of words, we have designed the material in a match-the-words format, so that by doing the exercises and checking the answers at the end of the book, you know the common meanings attached to these words without having to look up a dictionary.

Lest you forget, vocabulary building is not only about passing your English language paper; studies have shown that success in life, be it in school or at work, depends a great deal on your knowledge of words. Words are your tools to mastering other subjects — history, geography, science and so on. The larger your vocabulary, the greater your chances for success in life! For this reason, we have included numerous advanced-level words so that you are two notches above the average student in terms of reading and writing competence. If you can commit most of the words featured in this book to memory, you can be sure that you're on your way to success at reading and writing better!

By the time you finish this book, we hope to have fulfilled the following three aims:
1. Give you a rich source of essential words you should know by the time you sit for the GCE 'O' level English language examination.
2. Equip you with the necessary vocabulary skills to enhance your thinking and reading abilities.
3. Help you to appreciate the beauty and elegance of the English language and inspire you to dive deeper into the oceans of words to find more jewels of vocabulary.

You can tackle one or two units a day on your own or have fun doing the units with a friend or two. Remember, even after completing the units in this book, don't stop at it — continue to add new words to your vocabulary strongbox!

We hope you enjoy the book as much as we have in writing it!

Contents

Part 2   **Tackling the Vocabulary Question in the GCE 'O' Level English Language Paper 2**

Part 1

Building Your Vocabulary

Every word was once a poem.
Ralph Waldo Emerson

'Say' is a boring word if you use it all the time. So, before you use the word, pause and ask yourself whether another word can do a better job in conveying the tone or disposition of the speaker.

Choose the correct word to fill in each blank. Remember to use the correct form of the word.

acknowledge	declare	implore	object	protest

1. 'Let me go!' the human rights worker _____ angrily when the policeman locked her arms behind her back to subdue her.

2. 'I say we allocate $2 million for the project.'
    'That's too much,' _____ the director.

3. 'Please, return us our hard-earned money,' the investors _____.

4. 'It was not a good policy,' the minister _____ and promised to reverse the course of action.

5. 'I would rather resign than be coerced to commit a commercial crime,' he _____ when his boss persuaded him to join the scam.

announce	contend	pronounce	refute	suggest

6. 'My actions were sanctioned by the prime minister himself,' the colonel _____ when questioned relentlessly whether what he had done might be deemed criminally negligent.

7. 'The death toll is 91, and not 102, as you said,' the war minister _____ the director.

8. 'You're fit to resume duties,' the doctor _____.

9. 'Let's take a rest here before we proceed,' the guide _____, much to the relief of the hikers who were worn out from the walk.

10. 'There will be three months' bonus for employees,' the secretary _____.

claim	confess	proclaim	reiterate	rejoin

11. 'I was at the restaurant when the murder took place,' she _____.

12. 'I did it,' the woman finally _____.

13. 'The sixth of June shall be a national holiday in honour of the late president,' the prime minister _____.

14. 'Public funds should be channelled to saving lives and not wasted on space exploration,' he _____ throughout his speech, to much applause.

15. 'That's not a good idea,' he said.
'Well, do you have a better one?' she _____.

assert	counter	reason	stress	swear

16. 'We're above board in this matter. There's no fraud,' the CEO _____.

17. 'I'm going to make him pay for this!' she _____.

18. 'No, that's not what I was told to do,' he _____.

19. 'We must never — never — ignore the poor,' he _____.

20. 'I suppose prices will come down after the Christmas season since demand will be slack then,' he _____.

affirm	insist	lament	mutter	snort

21. 'Sir, is it true that the government will hold its election this year?'
'Yes,' the minister _____.

22. 'We have two serious health problems in the country. One is obesity and the other is inactivity,' _____ Dr John Bale.

23. 'I will only speak to the headmistress herself and no one else,' he _____.

24. 'What a stupid idea! Which idiot came up with it?' she _____.

25. 'I should have spoken up. I should have said I disagreed with all this,' she _____ to herself.

beg	complain	concede	demand	retort

26. 'I agree she's a good swimmer,' she _____. 'But I still think I can beat her in the swimming competition.'

27. 'Who did this?' he _____.

28. 'You stole it.'
'I certainly did not!' she _____.

29. 'Please don't do this!' she _____.

30. 'This is not my job, but the manager assigned it to me,' he _____.

 **Vocal Conveyance**

acknowledge — to accept, admit or recognise
affirm — to state that something is true
announce — to state or make known (usually publicly)
argue — to show disagreement
assert — to state, claim or establish forcefully
beg — to request strongly without pride
claim — to say that something is true
complain — to say that something is wrong or unsatisfactory
concede — to admit unwillingly
confess — to admit (usually regarding something wrong)
contend — to state as the truth
counter — to react with an opposing opinion
declare — to express clearly, firmly (often publicly)
defend — to protect against criticism
demand — to ask forcefully
exclaim — to say or shout something suddenly
implore — to ask in a determined and sincere way
insist — to demand forcefully, despite opposition
lament — to express sadness or regret
object — to express opposition to
plead — to make an urgent emotional request
pressure — to persuade to make sure something is accepted
proclaim — to announce publicly or officially (usually positive)
pronounce — to state officially, with certainty
protest — to express disagreement
rail — to complain angrily
rant — to shout angrily, often without meaning
reason — to understand and make judgements based on practical facts
rebuff — to refuse angrily
refute — to say or prove that something is wrong or false
reiterate — to say something again, or several times
rejoin — to give a quick answer, in an angry or amusing way
retort — to answer in an angry manner
screech — to exclaim loudly
snort — to express a strong feeling of impatience
suggest — to communicate or show without stating directly or giving proof
swear — to emphasise that something is true

Two office colleagues are describing their co-workers.

Complete the adjective that describes the people they are discussing by filling in the missing letters. Then think of two other adjectives that have the same meaning and write them in the blanks. You can choose these adjectives from the box on the next page.

1. You never know what he's going to do.

    u _ _ r e _ i _ _ _ a _ _ _ e

    _____

    _____

2. He never knows what he's going to do!

    _ n _ _ e c _ _ _ i _ _

    _____

    _____

3. You'd better watch what you say to him. Anything will set him off.

    _ e _ p _ _ _ a _ _ _ n t _ _

    _____

    _____

4. I never know what she's thinking.

    _ n s _ _ r _ _ t _ _ _ l _

    _____

    _____

5. If she likes you, she'll jump up, kiss you on the cheek and loudly declare it.

    e __ __ u __ __ v __

    _____

    _____

6. If she doesn't like you, she'll say so

    __ __ nd __ __

    _____

    _____

7. He never forgives a wrong; in fact, he'll make sure he finds a way of paying you back.

    __ i n __ __ c __ __ v __

    _____

    _____

8. He'll say what you want to hear, not what he really thinks.

    __ n __ __ n c __ r __

    _____

    _____

superficial	vengeful	volatile	irresolute
inconsistent	outspoken	malicious	capricious
glib	mercurial	frank	unrestrained
mysterious	demonstrative	unfathomable	hesitant

Unit 3   It's In The Attitude

Having an attitude is not a bad thing! You must have an attitude (fantastic, horrendous, chagrined, ardent, besotted) in order to write about something.

Below are 20 words (in bold) which you can use to show the way you look at things. For each word, circle the synonymous partner. How do you fare?

1. I told her **blatantly** that I did not like her bad attitude.
   (a) loudly   (b) intentionally   (c) rudely   (d) disrespectfully

2. I'm sure someone as self-possessed as Peter is **impervious** to her critical remarks.
   (a) disdainful   (b) scornful   (c) affected   (d) unconcerned

3. Beggars, diseased children and disconsolate women are **ubiquitous** in the slummiest part of the town.
   (a) unusual   (b) exceptional   (c) causing an eyesore   (d) omnipresent

4. The prime minister maintained an **intransigent** attitude towards public protest against the war, much to the mortification of the people.
   (a) unyielding   (b) accommodating   (c) open   (d) harsh

5. To her **chagrin**, the bus left just as she reached the bus stop.
   (a) rage   (b) acceptance   (c) annoyance   (d) indifference

6. He made some **desultory** remarks about his political opponents and incurred their wrath.
   (a) thoughtless   (b) irrelevant   (c) valid   (d) severe

7. The usually **stolid** Mary was in tears at the end of Roberto Benigni's movie *Life Is Beautiful*.
   (a) emotional   (b) impassive   (c) mischievous   (d) sharp-tongued

8. The minister's **feckless** handling of the water issue was widely criticised in the newspapers.
   (a) reckless   (b) unethical   (c) forceful   (d) incompetent

9. The lawyer's **cogent** arguments in court led her to win one of her greatest legal victories in her career.
   (a) convincing   (b) satisfying   (c) honest   (d) daring

10. Her **spurious** comments in the media about the scandal landed him in hot soup.
    (a) false   (b) true   (c) popular   (d) sharp

11. His placid nature belies his **penchant** for fast cars.
    (a) dislike   (b) disgust   (c) strong liking   (d) approval

12. Nobody appreciated the **deprecating** remarks.
    (a) offensive   (b) worthy   (c) credible   (d) thought-provoking

13. The police failed to assuage the anger of the **raucous** crowd of people and had to retreat.
    (a) unlawful   (b) angry   (c) noisy   (d) unpleasant

14. It is hard to believe that the successful man lived his youth in **insouciance**.
    (a) neglect   (b) excessiveness   (c) immorality   (d) carefreeness

15. He thought about her all day long and wrote **copious** poems about her.
    (a) lovely   (b) numerous   (c) mushy   (d) unimaginative

16. Not even the good news could lift his **lugubrious** mood.
    (a) angry   (b) depressing   (c) poignant   (d) sleepy

17. His **indomitable** spirit helps him overcome all the odds in his life.
    (a) cheerful   (b) liberal   (c) determined   (d) stubborn

18. She has a **capacious** appetite for learning new skills and acquiring knowledge.
    (a) small   (b) huge   (c) healthy   (d) excessive

19. You just don't know what to expect from that **capricious** woman.
    (a) mad   (b) funny   (c) strange   (d) unpredictable

20. The gifted but **impecunious** artist believed his paintings would sell only after his death.
    (a) humorous   (b) long-suffering   (c) poor   (d) eccentric

 Vocab List **Varying Attitudes**

ardent — showing strong, eager feelings
besotted — behaving unusually or foolishly as a result of being in love
blatant — obvious or intentional (usually negative)
capacious — able to contain a lot
capricious — tending to sudden and foolish changes
chagrin — frustration, marked by disappointment or humiliation
cogent — convincing or believable by virtue of forcible telling
copious — large and in great numbers
deprecating — expressing disapproval of
desultory — lacking in consistency or order
fantastic — highly impractical
feckless — without energy and enthusiasm
horrendous — extremely unpleasant
impecunious — poor, having little money
impervious — unable to be influenced
indomitable — difficult to defeat or frighten
insouciance — light and happy, acting without guilt
lugubrious — sad, in a slow way
penchant — a liking for something
raucous — noisy
spurious — false and not what it appears to be
stolid — showing little emotion or interest
ubiquitous — existing or found everywhere

One of the meanings of 'to cut' is to take apart or open up with a sharp tool. All the words in this unit have this general meaning.

A. **Fill in each blank with the most suitable word that represents a cutting action. Choose your words from the box below and use each word once only. Make sure the word you use is in the correct tense.**

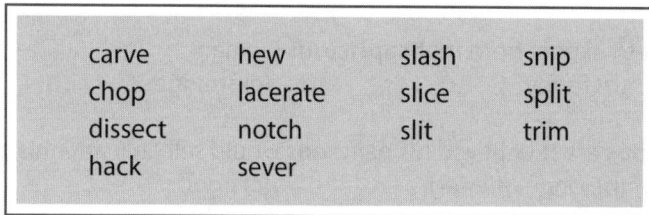

carve	hew	slash	snip
chop	lacerate	slice	split
dissect	notch	slit	trim
hack	sever		

1. The garden looks nice and tidy now that the gardener has mown the lawn and _____ the hedges.

2. I returned to my hotel room to find that someone had _____ the mattress and pillows in search of the missing letter.

3. The students are all excited as they will be _____ a frog for the first time today during their biology class.

4. The boy scouts are busy _____ logs for the campfire tonight.

5. With one swift stroke of his axe, the executioner _____ the head of the young queen.

6. The stranger _____ a wooden horse out of the old driftwood and gave it to the little boy.

7. Next, _____ the red peppers and add them to the soup.

8. Our native guide _____ away at the thick undergrowth with his machete.

9. The chef _____ the onions into round thin rings before coating them in batter.

10. I _____ off the corner of the carton and poured the milk into the saucer for my cat.

11. The man _____ the trees with a penknife as he went deeper into the jungle so that he would not get lost.

12. We could see in the distance the vague image of a face _____ out of the granite cliff.

13. His arms were badly _____ in his attempt to ward off the guard dog.

14. She _____ the envelope open with her letter opener, took out the note inside and read it quickly.

B. **Now that you have finished Part A above, you may have a better idea of the specific meaning of the 'cut' words. Match each word with its correct meaning.**

1. to carve

2. to chop

3. to dissect

4. to hack

5. to hew

6. to lacerate

7. to notch

8. to sever

9. to slash

10. to slice

11. to slit

12. to snip

13. to split

14. to trim

a. to roughly cut into pieces with a knife or axe

b. to make a long, narrow cut

c. to separate from the main part of something by a short, sharp cut

d. to divide with a cut along the grain

e. to cut with small, quick cuts, usually with scissors

f. to remove unnecessary material by cutting

g. to make small, V-shaped cuts

h. to cut into thin pieces

i. to cut a large piece out of a hard material

j. to make something by cutting into the surface

k. to make rough, repeated attempts to cut

l. to make a cut with a violent stroke

m. to take something apart to study its structure

n. to cut thin slices from a large piece of meat

o. to tear roughly, especially flesh

Think

Have you noticed that there seems to be one extra meaning? In fact, one of the words has two meanings. Which one do you think it is?

Vocab List **To Cut**

carve — to make something by cutting
chop — to sever with a single or series of blows
dissect — to cut apart in order to examine
engrave — to mark on a surface
hack — to cut with irregular blows
hew — to cut a large piece out of a hard material
incise — to cut into with a sharp instrument
lacerate — to cut or tear roughly
nick — to cut into
notch — to cut as a mark
score — to make a mark on a hard surface
scrape — to cut the surface of
sever — to separate from a whole
slash — to cut swiftly or violently
slice — to cut, usually to divide into pieces
slit — to make a long narrow cut
snip — to cut with one or two quick motions
split — to separate into portion(s)
trim — to reduce to a required length or state
whittle — to form a shape by removing bits off

Unit 5 Short And Sweet

A. The following is a list of words which are adjectives meaning 'short' or 'brief'. However, the list has many gaps. Complete the list by filling in the missing letters.

1. a b b r e v i [ ] [ ] d

2. a [ ] [ ] [ ] [ ] [ ] d

3. a b r [ ] [ ] t

4. b [ ] [ ] [ ] [ ]

5. b [ ] r [ ] q u e

6. c o [ ] [ ] s e

7. c o n [ ] [ ] s e d

8. c r [ ] [ ] p

9. c [ ] [ ] t

10. e c o n o m i [ ] [ ] [ ]

11. e p i [ ] [ ] [ ] m a t i c

12. i n c i [ ] [ ] [ ] [ ]

13. l a [ ] [ ] i c

14. m o [ ] [ ] s y l l a b i c

15. p [ ] [ ] h y

16. [ ] [ ] [ ] n t e d

17. s u c c [ ] [ ] c t

18. s u m [ ] [ ] i s e d

19. | t | a | c | i | | | |

20. | t | | | s | e |

21. | t | r | e | n | c | h | | | |

22. | t | r | u | n | | | | e | d |

B. Fill in each blank with a suitable word from the above list which matches the description below. The first two letters of each word have been given.

1. using words in a careful and concise way without wasting any   ec_____

2. stating facts or opinions in a strong and clever manner   pi_____

3. not speaking much, which makes you seem unfriendly   ta_____

4. using few words, often showing annoyance   te_____

5. using few words, unintentionally seeming rude   br_____

6. used for remarks which are very clear and direct, and which deal with the subject matter at hand   in_____

7. a shortened book   ab_____

8. a paragraph which contains only the main points   su_____

9. expressed briefly but clearly and effectively   su_____

10. short and witty in expression   ep_____

A good way to learn vocabulary words or to memorise their meanings is to learn to make meaningful sentences with them and give each word a context.

Examples:
- The prime minister was restrained in his speech, limiting his comments to a few *pithy* remarks on the inevitability of conflict with his long-time ally.
- Instead of saying a *succinct* goodbye, I fear I will engage in a long, teary scene at the airport with friends and family members.
- Steven's *trenchant* observations on Spielberg's movies were quite insightful and to the point — I never considered the director's methodology in that light before.

Now choose five words from the rest of the words you learnt in this unit and make a sentence each.

_____

_____

_____

_____

_____

_____

_____

_____

_____

_____

Light-Hearted And Fancy-Free

Compound adjectives are adjectives made up of two words. For example, in the sentence 'I feel quite *light-headed* suddenly; I must have had a little too much to drink', *light-headed* is a compound adjective which means 'feeling like you're about to lose consciousness' but in a different context it can also mean 'silly' or 'lacking seriousness' as in 'You can't rely on my *light-headed* sister — she only knows how to shop and have a good time.'

All these compound adjectives are formed from parts of the body. Fill in each blank with the correct compound adjective from the list on the next page.

1. My little sister is so _____ — she'll bring home every stray cat or dog if you give her half a chance.

2. Tiffany is your stereotypical _____ blonde — there's nothing in that pretty head of hers but clothes and jewellery.

3. My brother is quite a _____ chap — he'll go rushing headlong into trouble without a second thought.

4. Everyone at the meeting was required to come into the room _____ , then made to sit _____ on the floor.

5. The _____ serial killer was only caught three years after a victim had survived and identified him.

6. My boss is so _____ that he won't even replace the ten-year-old printer.

7. The bouncer tossed the loud, _____ drunk out of the bar after his cursing and swearing got out of control.

8. I don't think _____ men should wear suspenders with their trousers — it's certainly not a pretty sight!

9. These small-town people are so _____ and fixed in their ways; you're wasting your time trying to change things around here.

10. I tried to sell my homemade cookies at the fair but came home _____ — seems like no one likes lemon-grass-scented peanut cookies!

11. None of the employees likes Mr Chan because of his overbearing, _____ ways — I think this is one Boss's Day that'll go unnoticed.

12. After boasting about their son so much, Mr and Mrs Oon were _____ when he was caught _____ with the stolen items.

13. She's so _____ — she's always boasting!

14. He told a _____ lie when he claimed that I had spread the rumour about the company closing down.

15. 'Don't run around _____, Tommy, or you'll catch a cold,' Mrs Todd told the child.

hot-headed	tight-fisted	narrow-minded	feather-brained	bare-chested
foul-mouthed	soft-hearted	bald-faced	red-faced	bare-footed
cold-blooded	big-headed	cross-legged	empty-handed	pot-bellied
high-handed	red-handed			

Compound Adjectives

bald-faced — brash, undisguised
bare-chested — without clothing on the upper body (applicable more to men)
bare-footed — lack of footwear
big-headed — overly conceited or arrogant
cold-blooded — without emotion or feeling
cross-legged — sitting with legs placed one over the other
feather-brained — silly, empty headed
foul-mouthed — using abusive language
high-handed — arrogant, overbearing
hot-blooded — passionate, excitable
hot-headed — rash, easily angered
narrow-minded — not receptive, conservative
pot-bellied — having a protruding belly
single-minded — having a single aim or purpose, resolute
soft-hearted — generous in spirit
strong-armed — resorting to force
tight-fisted — stingy, unwilling to part with things

Complete the crossword puzzle and do a little better in the game of love! All you have to do is follow the clues. Good luck!

ACROSS

2 He should be less acquiescent and not let his wife rule under her _____.

4 How can you fall for another woman when you're married? That's _____ love!

8 Catherine is an irresistibly attractive woman. Half the men she meets worship her. I wish I were a femme _____ like her!

9 The sight of his old _____ stirred up memories of their love before they broke up.

11 There is still much _____ love between the couple after 50 years of marriage.

12 Beware! He's a _____, so you're not his only girlfriend.

14 Mrs Todd complained to her friend that there was no _____ in her marital life after ten years of marriage.

16 He's such a _____ — many girlfriends has he but none is he willing to marry.

17 Lucky you! Your Romeo is going to _____ you with a romantic song again.

19 He's my best friend — he's married and I've only _____ love for him.

20 Her love bordered on _____; why else would she stalk him?

DOWN

1 What a beautiful wedding dress! So when is the _____ day?

3 A two-_____ he is — he's seeing someone else other than you.

5 She can't do anything without him — she's definitely _____!

6 After being away from her husband for three months, she was beginning to _____ to be with him again.

7 He knows he's attractive. He's always after women and they all fall for his charms. He's such a Don _____.

10 Believe me — it's a case of _____ and not real love as you hardly know him.

13 'The _____ will be escorting you two until you are properly married,' the girl's mother pronounced.

15 Poor Jane! Her love was not only _____, but spurned.

18 Those two seem to like each other. I think I'll play _____ and hopefully, they'll be a couple soon.

 **Romance!**

ardour — great warmth of feeling
Casanova — man amorously and gallantly attentive to women
conjugal — relating to married persons and their relationships
chaperone — one who accompanies/supervises a woman
Don Juan — man who is an obsessive seducer of women
femme fatale — an attractive woman who often leads men into danger/dangerous situations
infatuation — an object of extravagant, short-lived passion
nuptial — of or pertaining to marriage/the marriage ceremony
platonic — relationship with the opposite sex without physical desire
philanderer — man who engages in many love affairs, usually with a casual attitude
romantic — expressing strong affection
serenade — performance given to express love for someone
spurn — to reject with disdain
unrequited — not returned or reciprocated
yearn — to have an earnest, strong desire

Haul Someone Over The Coals

A soldier disregarding his superior's orders is likely to get more than a scolding from his superior who is likely to reproach, rebuke or censure him for insubordination.

Unscramble the following words which are synonyms of 'scold' but with different intensities. Write the words in the blanks provided. Do not move the letters in bold.

1. The state coroner **bl**tsa**ed** the police officer's lack of vigilance and found him responsible for the victim's death through his negligence.

2. The prime minister **ca**tagits**ed** two of his ministers for their involvement in the scandal, which he said could hurt the credibility of his government.

3. The lieutenant was **l**ma**bs**a**ted** for abusing the prisoners under his charge.

4. The education minister was li**fi**v**ied** by the press for his latest proposal, which did not go well with the public.

5. The eminent scientist was ir**li**o**pl**ed by the science community for fabricating the research paper.

6. He kr**be**u**ed** his subordinates for falsifying the accounts in order to 'enhance' the sales reports.

7. The public **b**tae**red** the television company for screening excessively violent movies during peak family hours.

8. The parents h**d**i**ced** the child for playing truancy in school.

9. The judge **aim**shond**ed** the witness for failing to answer the question.

10. The employees were **v**e**or**p**red** for wastage such as throwing away good paper instead of recycling it.

11. The principal ar**p**iem**rd**n**ed** the pupils for spray-painting the walls.

12. The military court **c**nsreu**ed** the soldier for AWOL, that is, absence without official leave.

13. The judge i**hs**at**sc**ed the lawyer for his verbal outbursts in court.

14. Colin was **hu**rna**ga**ed by Professor Todd for failing to hand in his paper before the term started.

1. _____
2. _____
3. _____
4. _____
5. _____
6. _____
7. _____

8. _____
9. _____
10. _____
11. _____
12. _____
13. _____
14. _____

 **Vocab List** **To Scold**

admonish — to scold in a mild manner
berate — to scold angrily at length
blast — to scold in a critical and angry manner
castigate — to criticise someone severely
censure — to express official disapproval of
chastise — to scold severely
chide — to express disapproval of
criticise — to find fault with
harangue — to give a long, intense verbal attack
lambaste — to criticise severely, usually in public
lecture — to scold at length
pillory — to ridicule
rebuke — to express sharp disapproval of
reprimand — to scold (usually by a person of authority)
reprove — to correct
upbraid — to tell someone angrily of their wrongdoing
vilify — to spread negative information about

Ready To Wear

Do you know the names of these items of clothing? Fill in the blank spaces with the correct letters to make up the words.

1. A woollen hood covering the head and neck worn as protection against the cold.

   __ a __ a c __ a __ __

2. A round, flat cap usually made of felt or wool.

   __ e __ e __

3. It's the fashion these days to wear this large, printed handkerchief around the head.

   __ a __ d __ __ a

4. You will need this to keep you warm if you are in Alaska.

   p __ __ k __

5. The native Indians in Chile wear this — it's a blanket-like cloak with a slit in the middle for the head.

   __ o __ c __ o

6. The men of ancient Rome wore this loose, one-piece garment.

   __ __ g __

7. A band of fabric worn around the neck like a tie and tucked into the shirt.
   c __ a __ a __

8. Men wear this as part of formal evening wear — it's a kind of broad sash worn around the waist.
   __ u __ __ e __ __ u __ d

9. A form of protective clothing which workmen wear.
   __ __ e __ a __ __ s

10. A type of sweater with buttons down the front.
    c __ __ d __ __ a __

11. A sleeveless garment worn by men over their shirts as part of a three-piece business suit.
    __ a __ s __ __ o __ t

12. This is the American term for the garment in Question 11 above.
    __ e __ t

13. A man's dress jacket, usually worn for formal occasions.
    __ __ x __ d __

14. A square or rectangular piece of cloth worn draped around the shoulders.
    __ h __ w __

Opposites Do Not Attract

Do you know someone who is utterly boring? Someone so devoid of interest, so humdrum, dreary, monotonous and wearisome that just listening to him or her puts you to sleep? On the other hand, some people instantly liven things up wherever they are — they are lively, spirited, fascinating, vivacious, scintillating.

Look at the adjectives in the box below and put them under the correct headings.

indolent	overbearing	presumptuous	languorous
unpretentious	sedulous	modest	obsequious
self-effacing	supercilious	lackadaisical	pompous
diligent	unobtrusive	lofty	lowly
submissive	assiduous	commonplace	lethargic
unassuming	menial	disdainful	insignificant
sluggish	cocky	industrious	torpid
servile	laid-back	unproductive	cavalier
persevering	pretentious	egotistical	obscure
self-important	apathetic	differential	studious
high-handed	unflagging	vainglorious	languid
indefatigable	shiftless	painstaking	imperious
unrelenting	complacent	slothful	idle

Hardworking	Lazy	Proud	Humble

Animals Unite!

You probably already know common collective nouns for animals such as a *brood* of hens, a *litter* of pups and a *swarm* of bees. But do you know not-so-common collective nouns for our feathered acquaintances such as crows and amphibious creatures such as toads?

A. **Here's a jamboree of 'officially recognised' names for collective nouns in the animal kingdom. Choose a word from the list for each phrase (use each word once only).**

watch	unkindness	trip	team
string	smack	sloth	skulk
skein	siege	shrewdness	rye
run	rout	rafter	pride
pod	plague	pitying	peep
pace	parliament	paddling	ostentation
nest	mute	mustering	murmuration
murder	mob	leash	leap
labour	knot	kindle	kennel
husk	hover	host	gam
gaggle	field	exaltation	dule
drove	drift	dray	destruction
descent	deceit	crash	cowardice
covey	convocation	congregation	company
colony	clutter	cluster	clowder
cloud	charm	cast	business
building	barrel	bale	raft
army			

1. a _____ of ants
2. a _____ of apes
3. a _____ of asses
4. a _____ of bears
5. an _____ of caterpillars
6. a _____ of cats
7. a _____ of cats
8. a _____ of cattle
9. a _____ of chickens
10. a _____ of crows
11. a _____ of curs
12. a _____ of dogs
13. a _____ of doves
14. a _____ of ducks
15. a _____ of ducks (in water)
16. a _____ of eagles
17. a _____ of ferrets

18. a _____ of foxes
19. a _____ of geese
20. a _____ of geese (in flight)
21. a _____ of goats
22. a _____ of goldfinches
23. a _____ of grasshoppers
24. a _____ of greyhounds
25. a _____ of hares
26. a _____ of hawks
27. a _____ of herons
28. a _____ of hogs
29. a _____ of hounds
30. a _____ of housecats
31. a _____ of jellyfish
32. a _____ of kangaroos
33. a _____ of kittens
34. a _____ of lapwings
35. an _____ of larks
36. a _____ of leopards
37. a _____ of lions
38. a _____ of locusts
39. a _____ of moles
40. a _____ of monkeys
41. a _____ of nightingales
42. a _____ of owls
43. a _____ of oxen
44. a _____ of parrots
45. a _____ of partridges
46. an _____ of peacocks
47. a _____ of pheasants
48. a _____ of plovers
49. a _____ of ponies
50. a _____ of poultry
51. a _____ of racehorses
52. an _____ of ravens
53. a _____ of rhinoceroses
54. a _____ of rooks
55. a _____ of seals
56. a _____ of sparrows
57. a _____ of squirrels
58. a _____ of starlings
59. a _____ of storks
60. a _____ of toads
61. a _____ of trout
62. a _____ of turkeys
63. a _____ of turtledoves
64. a _____ of turtles
65. a _____ of vipers (snakes)
66. a _____ of whales
67. a _____ of wildcats
68. a _____ of wolves
69. a _____ of woodpeckers

B. **The adjectives on the left below are used to show that someone is like a certain animal. For example,** *canine* **means 'like a dog':** *The beast had canine teeth.* **Match each adjective with the animal.**

1.	aquiline		a.	viper
2.	asinine		b.	bear
3.	avian		c.	wild beast
4.	bovine		d.	ass
5.	canine		e.	hog
6.	corvine		f.	monkey
7.	elephantine		g.	cattle
8.	equine		h.	bird
9.	feline		i.	crow
10.	ferine		j.	fox
11.	formic		k.	ant
12.	leonine		l.	fish
13.	lupine		m.	horse
14.	viperine		n.	eagle
15.	ovine		o.	dog
16.	piscine		p.	elephant
17.	porcine		q.	lion
18.	ophidian		r.	cat
19.	simian		s.	sheep
20.	taurine		t.	wolf
21.	ursine		u.	snake
22.	vulpine		v.	bull

Think

1. English is a language which allows creativity. Invent some collective nouns of your own: a symphony of swallows, a parade of penguins, a convoy of zebras.

2. Make your characters come alive by likening them to an animal. Use the list in B to describe a certain feature or characteristic that they have. If a person moves stealthily like a cat, how might you describe her movement? If a person's remarks hurt like a snake, how might you describe his or her criticisms? If a person has a stupid expression on her face, like a cow, how might you describe her facial expression? Learn to use such adjectives to make your characterisation interesting!

English contains an array of 'multi-coloured' words which brighten up the world we live in!

Complete the words which represent the colour stated or shades of it by filling in the first or last three letters. Notice how each word 'colours' the object more beautifully.

WHITE

__ __ __ **lky** water
__ __ __ **amy** paper
iv __ __ __ cloth
mi __ __ __ skin
__ __ __ **rly** teeth
__ __ __ **w-white** shoes

BLACK

eb __ __ __ skirt
i __ __ __ night
__ __ __ **-black** hair
__ __ __ **ch-black** sky
pit __ __ __ room
ra __ __ __ hair
sa __ __ __ skies

GREY

as __ __ __ face
__ __ __ **y** cheeks
charc __ __ __ skin
ciner __ __ __ dusk
ho __ __ __ beard
__ __ __ **per-and-salt** complexion
__ __ __ **very-grey** car
sl __ __ __ **-grey** floor
sm __ __ __ eyes
st __ __ __ **-grey** door

BROWN

aub __ __ __ hair
__ __ __ **ge** envelope
__ __ __ **nzed** shoulders
__ __ __ **stnut** table
__ __ __ **colate-brown** suit
ha __ __ __ eyes
__ __ __ **ki** pants
__ __ __ **ogany** wardrobe
__ __ __ **tard-coloured** cravat
oc __ __ __ desk
__ __ __ **set** evening
__ __ __ **ia-toned** photograph
ta __ __ __ shirt

PURPLE

laven __ __ __ curtain
li __ __ __ petticoat
__ __ __ **ve** sweater
tyr __ __ __ purple nails
__ __ __ **let** eyeshadow

BLUE

__ __ __ **amarine** light
az __ __ __ sky
__ __ __ **ulean** eyeliner
cob __ __ __ **blue** Volkswagon
__ __ __ **igo** belt
__ __ __ **y blue** jeans
pruss __ __ __ blouse
ro __ __ __ **blue** shorts
__ __ __ **phire** water
__ __ __ **quoise** eyes

RED

__ __ __ **gundy** lips
__ __ __ **roty** cheeks
co __ __ __ **red** fingernails
__ __ __ **mson** sunrise
mar __ __ __ miniskirt
r __ __ __ **-coloured** paper
__ __ __ **y-red** dress
__ __ __ **rlet** silk
__ __ __ **milion** tassels
w __ __ __ **-red** gloves

GREEN

__ __ __ **rald** bracken
l __ __ __ print
ol __ __ __ eyes
verd __ __ __ garden
__ __ __ **idescent** eyeshadow

YELLOW

bl __ __ __ hair
__ __ __ **ter-coloured** hat
__ __ __ **mium yellow** tie
chr __ __ __ **yellow** brightness
fla __ __ __ skin
__ __ __ **den** sunrise
__ __ __ **fron** jacket
__ __ __ **dy** hair

ORANGE

am __ __ __ headlights
__ __ __ **icot** scarf
copp __ __ __ skin
__ __ __ **ger** eyebrows
ochre __ __ __ sunlight
__ __ __ **gerine** morning

Think What is a green-eyed monster? What is the difference between being 'in the pink' and 'seeing red'? What is a purple passage?

Things That Go Bump In The Night

Don't you love a spine-chilling, blood-curdling, send-you-shrieking ghost story? The kind that makes your hair stand on end and causes you to imagine all sorts of unpleasant things lurking in the shadows? If you do, then this exercise is right up your street. If not, then make sure you have (human) company when you attempt this exercise!

A. How many words associated with ghosts do you know?

1. Give four synonyms for 'ghost' starting with an 's'.
   a. s __ __ __ t __ e
   b. s __ __ r __ __
   c. s p __ __ __ e
   d. s __ __ o __

2. Other words for 'ghost' include the following:
   a. p __ a __ t __ __
   b. b __ g __ __ __ a __
   c. a __ __ a __ i __ __ o __
   d. g __ __ u __
   e. w __ a __ __ __

3. Of course, to a scientist there is no such thing as ghosts. Instead they are
   p _____ p_____ to be investigated.

4. Here are some unique types of ghosts. Match the words on the left with their correct descriptions on the right.
   a. poltergeist   i. a ghostly double of a living person

   b. doppelganger   ii. a corpse revived by black magic

   c. vampire   iii. a noisy and mischievous ghost that makes objects fly about, causing disorder

   d. zombie   iv. a dead person who rises from the grave at night to suck the blood of the living

B. The following sentences are not about ghosts at all, although they use the idea of ghosts and death in the expressions. Fill in the blanks with the correct expressions using the clues in the brackets to help you.

1. When he has his earphones on, he is _____ (use four words, including the word 'dead'). He won't hear you even if you shout at him.

2. My cousin has to work the _____ (use two words, including the word 'graveyard') in the nursing home, so he is usually at home in the daytime sleeping.

3. This place has turned into a _____ (use two words, including the word 'ghost') ever since the copper mines closed down and most of the young people left to find new jobs in the city.

4. There isn't a _____ (use four words, including the word 'ghost') that he will win the gold medal now that he has torn his hamstring.

5. This subject has been _____ (use three words, including the word 'death') in the movies — I'm so sick of it.

6. Not many people are aware that my brother _____ (use one word containing the word 'ghost') for the famous actor Troy McLean. Troy can act, but he sure can't write!

7. The poor woman _____ (use four words, including the word 'ghost') when she saw her husband, whom she thought had died, walk into the room. She was literally scared to death!

8. She was so _____ (use two words, including the word 'dead') on leaving the company that she was prepared to resign without securing another job first.

9. It is common to have a _____ (use three words, including the word 'dead') in a train as a safety measure in case the driver is incapacitated in some way.

10. Every cigarette he smoked was another _____ (use four words, including the word 'coffin').

Get Around To Doing Away With

A phrasal verb is made up of a verb and a preposition or adverb. A lot of phrasal verbs are idiomatic. For example, in the sentence 'My brother is very good at *taking off* people — his impersonation of our principal never fails to entertain our friends', you can probably guess from the context that *taking off* means imitating. The phrasal verb *take off* is idiomatic because the meaning cannot be deciphered from the individual words; it has a meaning all its own, unlike the literal meaning of *take off* in a sentence like 'Take off your shoes before you step into the house'.

A. Fill in the blank with a suitable preposition/adverb to form the correct phrasal verb.

1. My Australian neighbour took _____ my mother the moment they met — they have been fast friends ever since.

2. The burglar made _____ with almost a quarter of a million dollars in cash and jewellery.

3. I don't think I can take _____ any more tonight — I've been studying for four hours straight.

4. Don't be taken _____ by his apparently easy-going manner — he'll be on you like a ton of bricks if you don't follow the rules.

5. Our teacher briefly touched _____ the topic; what he taught us wasn't enough to help us answer the question well.

6. My boss has given me the task of breaking _____ the new employee — I hope he's a fast learner because we're going to need him to help with our presentation next week.

7. I hope I'm not putting you _____ by dropping by unexpectedly like this.

8. I was put _____ by my date's disgusting eating habits — he kept burping and picking his teeth during the entire meal!

9. The milk has gone _____ — just pour it down the sink!

10. I'm afraid she never really gets _____ her father's death.

Breakthroughs And Breakouts

We looked at phrasal verbs in Unit 14. A number of phrasal verbs also act as compound nouns.

Here are some examples:
- She suffered a nervous *breakdown* right after she lost her job.
- Production *output* has increased this month — thanks to the new equipment.
- He received some positive *feedback* with regard to the publishing of her first cookbook.

A. Combine a verb in the left box with a preposition in the right box to form a compound noun. Either the verb or preposition can come first.

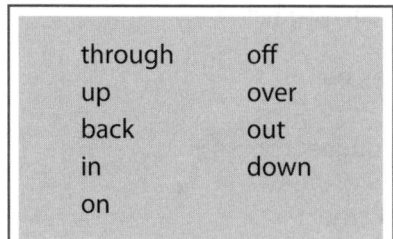

hang	lay
stand	cut
lie	fall
cover	hand
drive	draw
hold	turn
break	write
crack	shake
turn	walk
write	set

+

through	off
up	over
back	out
in	down
on	

B. Complete the following mini-crossword puzzles.

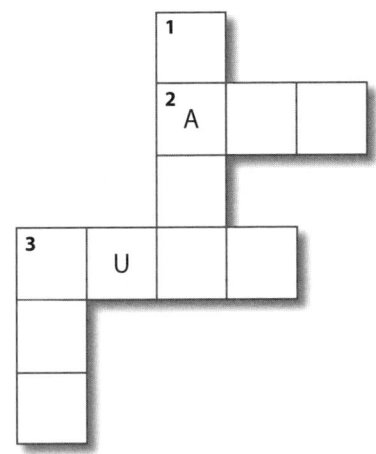

1 down: I didn't expect our holiday plans to _____ through at the last minute.

2 across: Are you sure you can manage the children? They tend to _____ up when they get bored.

3 across: Don't _____ out the possibility of going back to work full-time.

3 down: I dislike that woman — she always _____s down people behind their backs.

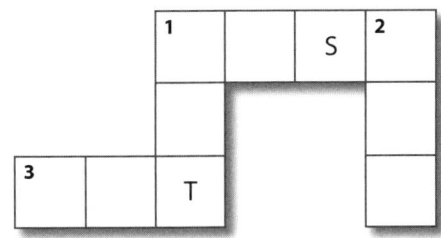

1 across: She can't possibly _____ up this job offer — it comes with an internship at the Boston office.

1 down: I've never seen a girl _____ on airs like Viji — how can you bear to be her friend?

2 down: I have to _____ about booking a hotel room for my boss. Any ideas?

3 across: He'll _____ around the rules somehow — he always does.

C. The following phrasal verbs are made up of three parts. See if you know what they are from the context of the sentences. The first letter of the verb is given to help you.

1. The new polytechnic has d_____ _____ _____ textbooks altogether. Students are supposed to do their own research and gather their own reading material.

2. We had to p_____ _____ _____ the noise from the renovation works next door.

3. Do you f_____ _____ _____ staying at the library after school to read up on our assignment? Or will you be too tired?

4. I don't know where he gets the energy — he must be g_____ _____ _____ 60 years, at least!

5. How can you suggest that we take a trip to Thailand without the wives — I don't g_____ _____ _____ that sort of thing!

6. Keiko has f_____ _____ _____ the marketing director. Now they hardly talk to each other.

7. He tried to d_____ his wife _____ _____ her inheritance but thankfully he didn't succeed.

8. Let's hope our boss doesn't g_____ _____ _____ her word to send us for the training package. She's been known to do just that.

15

The Good, The Bad …

All the adjectives listed below are synonymous with either 'good' or 'bad'. Put each word under the appropriate heading in the table below. There should be 16 words under each heading. One of each has been given as an example.

abysmal	apocryphal	baleful	benevolent
bona fide	consummate	debauched	detrimental
diabolical	duplicitous	egregious	flagrant
fraudulent	heinous	immaculate	impartial
impeccable	infernal	insidious	judicious
magnanimous	malevolent	meritorious	nefarious
odious	principled	scrupulous	seraphic
stupendous	sublime	unparalleled	veracious

Good	Bad
benevolent	abysmal

 **Vocab List** **Positive And Negative**

abysmal — extremely bad or severe
apocryphal — untrue but believed by some
baleful — having harmful intent
benevolent — expressing kindly feelings
bona fide — not false, real
consummate — complete in every way
debauched — corrupted
detrimental — harmful effect
diabolical — extremely bad and shocking
duplicitous — deceitful
egregious — extraordinary in a bad way
flagrant — shocking due to its obviousness
fraudulent — deceitful in order to gain power or money
heinous — shockingly evil
immaculate — free from fault or flaw
impartial — not biased
impeccable — perfect, undamaged by fault
infernal — extremely troublesome
insidious — gradually and secretly causing harm
judicious — showing good judgement in making decisions
magnanimous — very generous and honourable
malevolent — showing ill will
meritorious — deserving praise
nefarious — extremely wicked
nihilistic — lawless, ungoverned
odious — extremely unpleasant
principled — behaving in an honest way
scrupulous — extremely honest
seraphic — beautiful in a way that suggests goodness
stupendous — causing amazement
sublime — extremely good, beautiful or enjoyable
unparalleled — without equal
veracious — truthful, honest

Power-Packed Vocabulary for 'O' Level English

Unit 16 ... And The Ugly

The word 'ugly' doesn't affect us anymore. But say 'heinous' or 'vile' and you could send a chill down our spines. Learn to use the following adjectives for 'ugly' and make your listener shudder with revulsion!

While you're at it (learning the words and not making your listener shudder with revulsion), find all the words and circle them in the word square. The words appear horizontally (forwards and backwards), vertically and diagonally.

ARTLESS	EMACIATED	HIDEOUS	SCLEROTIC
ATROCIOUS	FARINACEOUS	LEPROUS	SINISTER
BOVINE	GAWKY	MACABRE	UNGAINLY
CADAVEROUS	GEEKY	PORCINE	UNPREPOSSESSING
DOWDY	GROTESQUE	REPUGNANT	VILE

```
B M E T T G E S E N I V O B C R A G N U
G L A Y F A R C I Y E T H I A N A N N U
G L Y C M I N O K N D J T I Z Q J I A G
B S G B A P I W T X I O W S C S O S M R
D O W D Y B A L I E R S U T U H L S I G
P H O M J G R X D E S O T O S Z E E F G
S U O E D I H E L S I Q R E B Q N S H E
K U U W D R E C U C X P U R R H S S C E
U N O W D J S O O D E P Z E Q N N O Y K
D N E I L B R R E L J G M B H W Y P Y Y
Z W G O D E T T E N I C R O P N L E W S
V Q H A V A A R H I Z I J J J Y J R T T
E X T A I I I T Q E L I V I M Q G P D N
K D D E C N D G O F I V I P L J P N S A
L A D A P Y L P I C J O A Y S M T U S N
C H M Y X K W Y C H X U H Z K Q U M E G
U E X W W E I E M W A C W L F V B H L U
A X W B K A F A R I N A C E O U S U T P
P T A W I F F V F R U O T T Q A T E R E
K U J J R S T F N A I F J E B T V U A R
```

What is the hidden quotation in the puzzle? Write the uncircled letters in the first three lines of the puzzle (left to right) in the blanks below. Do you know the author of this quotation?

——————— —— ————— ———— ————

—— ———— ————.

artless — poorly made, unskilful
atrocious — shockingly bad
bovine — dull
cadaverous — thin, haggard
dowdy — old-fashioned, therefore unattractive
emaciated — weak due to hunger
farinaceous — having a mealy, that is, dry and powdery, appearance
gawky — tall and awkward
geeky — person regarded as unfashionable and lacking in social skills
grotesque — unnatural in shape
hideous — very ugly
leprous — affected with leprosy
macabre — ghastly, horrible
porcine — resembling a pig
repugnant — distasteful
revolting — disgusting
sclerotic — hardened, stony in texture
sinister — threatening
ungainly — not graceful
unprepossessing — not impressive
vile — highly unpleasant

Make your character interesting. Don't tell the reader she's got nice hair when you mean she has a ballerina bun fastened down with an ornate steel hairpin, or a thick plait secured with a lilac elastic band. So give your character a head start by crowning her (or him) with hair, glorious hair!

A. Learn some hairstyle names by unscrambling the letters to reveal the hairstyles shown in the pictures.

1.   y a p b g e o

_____

2.   r z f i z

_____

3.   r e n g i f

_____

4.   A o f r

_____

5.   o f a b u n t f

_____

6.   o a w h m k

_____

7.   r a c d k d o l s e

_____

8.   d u r p p a o m o

_____

9.   p s k s e i

_____

B. Have a go at naming the following definitions related to hair. The first letter of each word is given to help you.

1. hairstyle   c _____

2. close-cropped hair, usually on man   c _____   c _____

3. windblown, uncombed hair   t _____

4. balding at the top of brow, causing the hairline to move back on crown   r _____   h _____

5. having short, neat hairstyle   c _____

6. abundant or long thick hair   m _____

7. person with totally shaved head   j _____ or s _____

8. hair formed into loose curls   w _____

9. hair cut all one length to shoulder or shorter   b _____

10. American word for 'plait'   b _____

Oops! I Meant To Say …

A malapropism is a word used incorrectly in place of another, often with hilarious results. For example, in the sentence 'He is a man of great statue', 'statue' is the malapropism — the correct word is 'stature'. The word 'malapropism' comes from a character called Mrs Malaprop in a comedy called *The Rivals* written by Richard Sheridan in the 18th century. She would say things like 'I am sure I have done everything in my power to explode the affair' and 'Promise to forget this fellow — to illiterate him from your memory!'. (What were the words she intended to use?)

Identify the malapropisms in the following letter and replace them with the correct words.

From: Yeo Soo Chen <yeosoochen@gmail.com>

Sent: Friday June 21, 2006, 2.06 PM

To: Jinny Chew <chewjinny@singnet.com.sg>

Subject: Invitation to Dinner Party

Dear Jinny

I'm throwing a small dinner party for a few elected friends this weekend. Do say you'll come! I know you don't like to show off, but this is the perfect opportunity to suppress the other guests with your expansive brocade dress — you know, the one that makes you look so svelte and ravenous.

I've invited three other couples and two 'singletons'. Perhaps the two will hit it off — Dan is a very illegible bachelor; he's a very nice fellow and runs his own design firm. The lady, Sok Chin, is a marvellous cook and a great conservationist — she can talk about anything under the sun and put you at your ease at once. I'm hoping she'll draw out the Tans who are quite a shy couple. They were at this party where the guests were quite a raucous bunch — much to the Tans' constipation. Oh yes, I've invited Nigel — he's always got a store of amusing antidotes. Must remember to bring the two dogs over to Mum's place, though — Nigel's wife is putrefied of canines.

The last couple are the Lims. As you know, they live in an effluent neighbourhood and Mr Lim talks about nothing but making money — he's always trying to make me infest in some unit trust or other. His wife is quite an auspicious woman, always giving unwanted advice. But despite all that, they mean no harm and are really quite a kind and helpful couple.

Just call me to confirm you'll be coming — don't bother to e-mail me back. I hope you don't mind me saying that it's rather painful to read your e-mails — your spelling is quite abdominal, you know!

Cheers
Soo Chen

B. Fill in the blank with the correct compound noun you have formed.

1. There will be a substantial number of _____ this year. Every manager is required to make assessments of his or her staff to decide who should go and who should stay.

2. The _____ on the sale of illegal software is beginning to have an effect — you can hardly find pirated DVDs anymore.

3. Make sure you have a _____ plan in case our initial plan doesn't work out.

4. The charity organisation is now engaging in damage control — trying to contain the _____ from the corruption scandal.

5. The unemployed man was too proud to receive the _____ of food and clothing from the organisation.

6. The new restaurant received a very good _____ in the papers.

7. The _____ flight revealed some flaws in the new guidance system.

8. The _____ at the concert was surprisingly good, considering the controversy surrounding the performer.

9. The prison _____ left a number of guards and inmates seriously injured. Eventually all the convicts were captured.

10. Discovering the drug that could treat leprosy was a real medical _____.

11. The mysterious disease resulted in the _____ of ageing well before his time — before long his hair had turned completely white, his skin began to sag, and his eyesight began to fail.

12. We were told right at the _____ that the merger would definitely take place this year.

13. The page _____ in this magazine is very chaotic — too many bright colours and hard-to-read fonts, and not enough white space.

14. The new venture required an initial _____ of close to half a million dollars.

For The Time Being

Study the following list of 15 words which are associated with things of a brief or temporal nature. Then cover the list and complete the words by filling in the missing letters. After completing each word, write it down in the blank. Take note of the nouns which it describes. Write down other nouns you come across which may aptly be described by the word.

cursory	fugacious	passing
ephemeral	fugitive	short-lived
episodic	impermanent	temporal
evanescent	interim	transient
fleeting	momentary	transitory

1. ep __ s __ d __ __   _____ *illness, attacks*

2. c __ rs __ r __   _____ *smile, kiss*

3. eph __ m __ r __ __   _____ *beauty, pain*

4. __ v __ n __ sc __ __ t   _____ *rash, itch*

5. m __ m __ __ t __ __ y   _____ *happiness, glimpse*

6. p __ s __ __ __ g   _____ *thoughts, showers*

7. f __ __ et __ __ g   _____ *glance, shadow*

8. __ __ __ rt- __ __ __ __ d   _____ *relationship, joys*

9. tr __ __ s __ __ nt   _____ *beauty, affection*

10. f __ g __ c __ ou __   _____ *blossoms, scent*

11. tr __ __ s __ t __ __ y   _____ *period, power*

12. __ mp __ __ m __ n __ __ t   _____ *wealth, love*

13. f __ g __ t __ __ __   _____ *thoughts, hours*

14. t __ __ p __ r __ l   _____ *existence, possessions*

15. __ nt __ __ __ m   _____ *agreement, report*

Keep It Simple

The words in this unit are not slick or impressive words; on the contrary, they embrace simplicity and unoriginality, to the extent of dullness. But this doesn't mean they're useless words! If you want to talk about ordinariness, you can use these not-so-ordinary words to say what you really mean.

Cross out three letters to unravel the word which fits the sentence.

1. | P | R | O | S | R | A | I | H | A | C |

   Mrs Cane commented that most of our essays about growing up were unimaginative and _____.

2. | T | P | E | D | R | E | S | W | T | R | I | A | N |

   Don't waste your money on the movie; the _____ plot will put you to sleep after 15 minutes!

3. | M | A | T | U | N | D | A | T | N | E |

   I'd be the last person on earth to write an interesting autobiography — my life is too _____!

4. | E | R | A | R | X | T | H | I | B | O | U | N | D |

   I lead quite an _____ existence. You'll never see me in dangerous pursuits such as bungee-jumping and skydiving; if I want excitement, I watch a thriller.

5. | B | A | N | O | A | T | L | A |

   Since there were many restrictions on the kinds of questions asked of the movie star, reporters asked the most _____ questions which had been asked and answered before.

6. | R | V | A | I | C | U | E | O | U | S |

   The politicians gave a lot of _____ ideas which lacked substance and workable solutions for the country's economic problems.

7. | I | T | N | E | A | N | B | E |

Holding a lottery to raise church funds? What an _____ suggestion!

8. | I | N | A | G | E | N | S | U | D | O | U | S |

The manager accepted the old man's _____ explanation that it was pure forgetfulness that he left the store without paying for the item.

9. | T | Q | U | I | O | T | I | R | D | I | A | N |

Bacon and eggs are _____ morning fare in bed-and-breakfast arrangements.

10. | T | E | R | I | O | T | E | R |

I tried to be original in the writing but ended up including many _____ clichés which I was sure Mrs Kimble would pick out.

11. | O | P | L | E | G | Q | B | E | I | A | N |

He holds no special rank, so you could say he is a _____ in the army.

12. | P | A | T | R | O | E | C | H | I | D | A | L |

Having lived in a small town all his life, he has _____ attitudes towards city life.

13. | S | O | A | P | O | U | R | I | F | I | C | A |

Gillian's _____ voice droned on, inducing a drowsy effect in all of us.

14. | G | U | E | I | L | E | L | E | S | O | S | M |

We were surprised at the shrewd way he dealt with the matter, which belied his seemingly _____ nature.

15. | M | E | A | L | D | I | U | O | C | R | E |

Her work performance is _____; I'm not impressed.

banal — boring and not original
earthbound — not exciting
guileless — honest (usually used to describe a person)
humdrum — lacking excitement
inane — lacking real meaning or importance
ingenuous — honest in a way that seems foolish
mediocre — not very good
mundane — very ordinary
parochial — showing interest in only a narrow range of matters
pedestrian — not interesting, showing little imagination
plebeian — of a low social class
prosaic — lacking interest, imagination and variety
quotidian — ordinary, everyday
soporific — causing a person to feel sleepy
tedious — uninteresting and tiring
trite — expressed too frequently to be interesting
vacuous — not expressing or showing intelligent thought
wearisome — causing a person to be tired or bored

Unit 22 Shape Up!

What makes the world such an interesting place are the myriad shapes that surround us. Learn as many names of shapes as you can so that you can be as precise in your description as possible when you describe something. To enhance your writing, use shapes as adjectives to describe items: a pyramid pendant, scallop edges, a tessellated table cloth. Each of the shapes gives a more vivid image of the object, doesn't it?

A. Write the name of the shape suggested by the picture to describe the object.

bulbous	hexagonal	serrated
conical	orbicular	spiral
corrugated	pretzel	tessellated
cuneate	prism	toothed
elliptic	reticulated	trifurcated
funnel	scallop	tubular

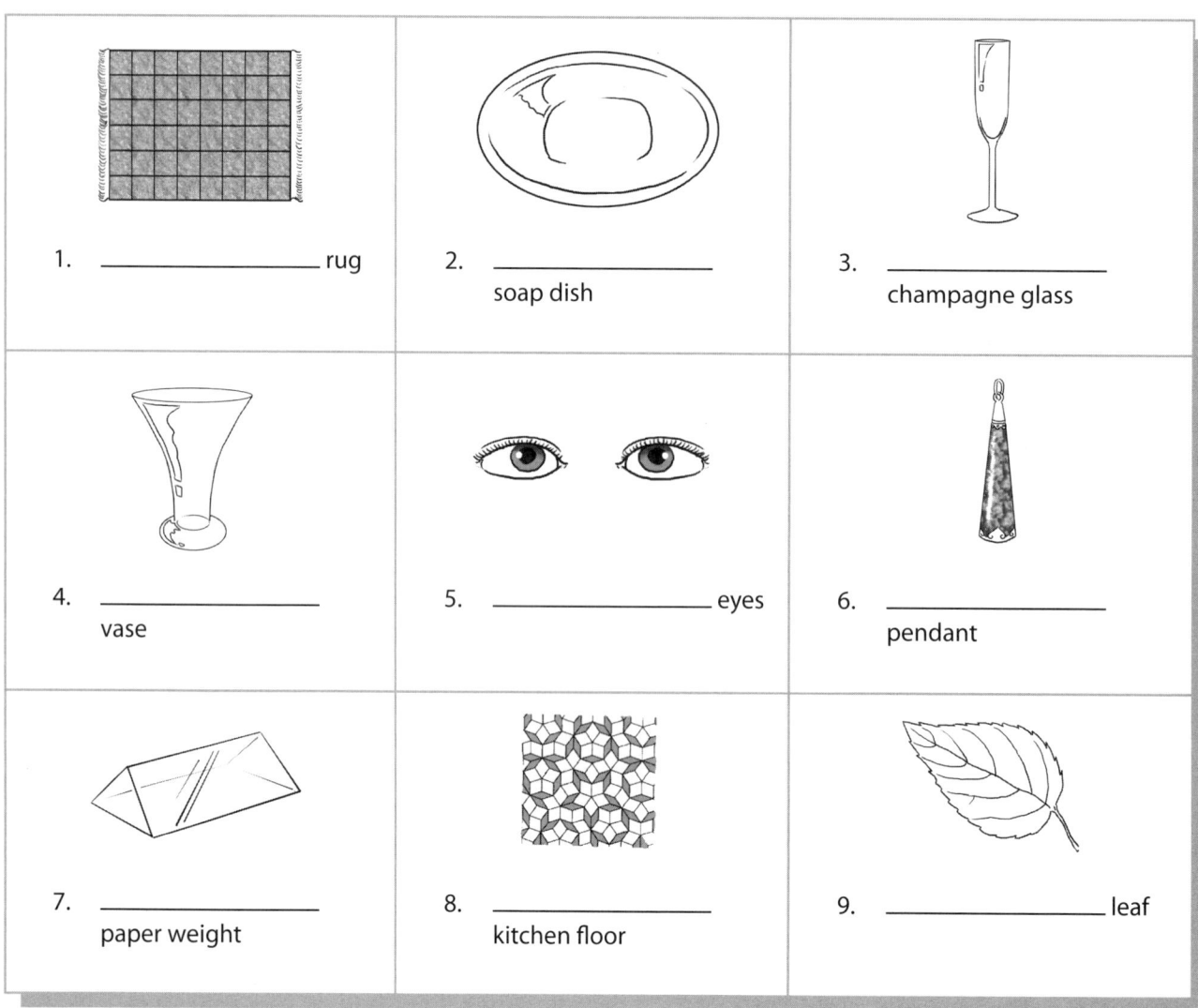

1. _____ rug

2. _____
   soap dish

3. _____
   champagne glass

4. _____
   vase

5. _____ eyes

6. _____
   pendant

7. _____
   paper weight

8. _____
   kitchen floor

9. _____ leaf

10. _____ fan

11. _____
staircase

12. _____ edge

13. _____
tile

14. _____ bowl

15. _____
candle stand

16. _____ -
shaped accessory pin

17. _____ -
shaped Chinese vase

18. _____ iron
sheet

B. Match each word to its correct definition.

acicular	cordate	stellate
amorphous	furrowed	trihedral
bacillary	palmate	undulating
campanulate	protuberant	whorl

1. heart-shaped _____
2. needle-shaped _____
3. something that whirls, coils or spirals _____
4. grooved _____
5. shapeless _____
6. having a rolling appearance like waves _____
7. having three faces _____
8. bulging out _____
9. bell-shaped _____
10. rod-shaped _____
11. star-shaped _____
12. having the appearance of a hand with fingers spread _____

In Unit 20, we looked at words related to time of a temporal nature. In this unit, we shall look at 15 words associated with words synonymous with 'permanent'.

Again, study the list of words first. Then, without referring to the list, try to complete each word on your own before writing it down in the blank. Write down other nouns you come across which may aptly be described by that word.

ageless	incessant	prolonged
amaranthine	infinite	relentless
eternal	interminable	timeless
immortal	perennial	unceasing
immutable	perpetual	unflagging

1. e t e r _ _ _ _   _____ *wait, truth*

2. _ m m _ t _ b _ _   _____ *view, standpoint*

3. _ m m _ _ t _ _   _____ *words, fame*

4. p _ _ p _ t _ _ l   _____ *complaints, pain*

5. i n t _ _ _ m _ n _ b l _   _____ *wait, stay*

6. p _ r _ n n _ _ _ _   _____ *sadness, happiness*

7. i _ f _ n _ t _   _____ *care, wisdom*

8. i _ c _ s s _ _ _ t   _____ *rain, noise*

9. r _ l _ _ _ t l _ _ s   _____ *pursuit, effort*

10. u n c _ _ _ s _ _ g   _____ *love, faith*

11. _ n f _ _ g g _ _ g   _____ *kindness, spirit*

12. _ m _ r _ _ _ t h _ _ _ _   _____ *beauty, calm*

13. t _ _ _ _ l _ _ s   _____ *design, lessons*

14. p r _ l _ _ _ g _ d   _____ *illness, sorrow*

15. _ g e _ _ s _   _____ *fascination with the theme of good and evil, questioning the origin of life*

A. Human beings are quite a critical lot, judging by the numerous words in the vocabulary used for lashing out at other people. Look at the words in the box on the next page. They are all synonymous with the word 'criticise'. Spend about two minutes studying the words before filling them in the blanks. Use the correct form of the word. We've given you clues for each word, so this one should be a cinch!

1. The public _____ the use of force in settling the conflict between the two states. (8 letters beginning with 'd')

2. The human rights group _____ the abuse of prisoners detained in the military camp. (7 letters with 'c')

3. Poor Joe! All his classmates _____ him for wearing a lime green shirt with mismatched maroon socks to school. (7 letters beginning with 'd')

4. The dictator was _____ for his atrocities against his countrymen during his rule. (9 letters beginning with 'c')

5. The actress's new play was _____ by the critics for its amoral themes. (9 letters with 2 'a's)

6. The opposition leaders _____ the use of public funds to support the government's next election campaign. (9 letters with 2 'n's)

7. She tends to _____ her own efforts. (8 letters beginning with 'b')

8. The couple _____ the lack of decent facilities in the out-of-the-way hotel. (8 letters with 'o')

9. His latest architectural design was widely _____ by critics. (10 letters beginning with 'd')

10. The public _____ the board's idea of building a modern shopping mall in the middle of the heritage park. (9 letters with 2 'i's)

11. Unlike his previous movies, the latest motion picture by the acclaimed director has been much _____ by the media. (8 letters beginning with 'm')

12. The film was _____ by critics for its excessive violence and crude language. (6 letters beginning with 'r')

13. Women in that country are still being _____ by men as being the weaker sex. (10 letters with 'n' and 't')

14. 'You're a good-for-nothing coward,' she _____ him. (7 letters with 'u')

15. In his speech, the politician _____ against capital punishment and called for abolition of the death penalty. (10 letters beginning with 'f')

16. The tabloids were _____ by the government for their sensational reporting of the scandal involving the president. (7 letters beginning with 's')

17. Her play was _____ by the critics for poor dialogue and amateurish acting. (6 letters beginning with 'p')

18. The rights activist _____ against the indiscriminate killing of children and women in the genocide. (9 letters with 'v' and beginning with 'i')

19. Her boss _____ her in front of all her colleagues. (10 letters beginning with 'h')

20. He put up a first-rate performance which could not be _____. (7 letters beginning with 'f')

belittle	deride	malign
bemoan	disparage	pan
condemn	fault	rap
decry	fulminate	ridicule
denigrate	humiliate	slam
denounce	inveigh	taunt
deplore	lambaste	

B. Divide the words in the box into three categories. There are five words in each group. Note: One word is an oddball which does not belong in any of the three groups.

absolve	exculpate	reproach
acquit	execrate	reprobate
censure	exonerate	revile
curse	indict	vindicate
deprecate	remonstrate	vituperate
excoriate		

To disapprove or blame	To condemn or criticise abusively	To clear from blame

C. Fill in the sentence below with the oddball.

The salesgirl only allowed the refund after Jason started to _____ with her.

Do you remember what a malapropism is? Here are more examples of interesting kinds of expressions.

Match each expression with its meaning, and then its example.

1.	anagram	a sentence that uses every letter of the alphabet	'The quick sharp scratch and blue spurt of a lighted match'
2.	spoonerism	misuse of a word in place of one that sounds like it, often with amusing results	'If you intend to use PHP for command line scripting, you always need the command line executable.'
3.	malapropism	a milder expression instead of a harsh or offensive one	'Never odd or even'
4.	palindrome	the specialised or technical expressions of a particular field or profession	'sanitation worker' = 'garbage man'
5.	mnemonic	a word or phrase in which the letters or syllables get swapped	'A lack of pies' = 'A pack of lies'
6.	acronym	a combination of contradictory words	'Life is far too important a thing ever to talk seriously about.'
7.	euphemism	a word or phrase that reads the same forwards and backwards	'He is the very pineapple of politeness!'
8.	onomatopoeia	a witty, often paradoxical remark	'genuine imitation' and 'original copies'
9.	pangram	a word formed from the first letters of another word	'The quick brown fox jumps over the lazy dog.'
10.	oxymoron	a word or phrase formed by changing the sequence of letters of another	'V I Boys Get Your Orange Ready!' = The colours of the rainbow (Violet, Indigo, Blue, Green, Yellow, Orange, Red)

| 11. jargon | a sentence that is supposed to help one remember things | 'Desperation' = 'A rope ends it' |
| 12. epigram | the use of words that imitate sounds | 'WYSIWIG' = What you see is what you get |

Power-Packed Vocabulary for 'O' Level English

In this exercise we will focus on idiomatic expressions consisting of two words joined with the conjunction *and* or *or*. Some examples include cut *and* dried, odds *and* ends, give *or* take.

A. **Pick a word from the box on the right to combine with the word on the left (which should come first) to form the correct expression. You will not use all the words in the box.**

1. cut and _____
2. wine and _____
3. law and _____
4. nuts and _____
5. down and _____
6. sixes and _____
7. blood and _____
8. nook and _____
9. thick and _____
10. prim and _____
11. spick and _____
12. rack and _____

seeds	proper	order
tack	run	wet
bolts	speck	in
neat	thunder	dine
cranny	long	bread
out	sewn	retribution
tidy	ruin	span
fat	lightning	centre
eights	thin	sevens

B. **Fill in the blanks with the correct words.**

1. My boss has been keeping me busy running all sorts of errands. I've been at her _____ and _____ all morning.

2. The Miller siblings may be fraternal twins but they're as different as _____ and _____.

3. The student got very low marks for her term paper because it was just _____ and _____ — all she did was cobble together texts she had read from a few websites.

4. The public raised a great _____ and _____ over the wrong suspect being shot by the police.

5. I'm glad to hear that Kim is getting better and is already _____ and _____, doing all the things she enjoys doing.

6. For a moment it was _____ and _____ whether the accident victim would live, but he managed to pull through at last.

7. At first he was calm and collected at the press interview, but as the questions came at him _____ and _____, he lost his temper and yelled at the reporters.

8. There were several accusations of him cheating in the race, but the judges ruled that he had won it _____ and _____.

9. I'm _____ and _____ of your constant complaints about your roommate — why don't you just move?

10. During my first week on the job, I was left to _____ or _____. Everybody was too busy to teach me the ropes and give me a helping hand.

11. She refused to make any compromise regarding the situation: it was _____ or _____.

12. Be patient — _____ or _____ you will be promoted if you work hard.

C. What is the difference between the expressions 'give-and-take' and 'give or take'? Which would be the correct expression to use for each of the following sentences?

1. Marriage involves both partners making a lot of compromises.

2. There were approximately 300 people at the seminar.

The words you see in this exercise contain at least four syllables — in other words, they are l – o – n – g.

A. Match the words with their meanings.

1.	gobbledygook	a.	the ringing of bells, a jingling or tinkling sound
2.	pusillanimous	b.	discovering something purely by chance
3.	flabbergasted	c.	indescribable, incapable of being expressed
4.	serendipitous	d.	incomprehensible or nonsense words, or wordy and unintelligible jargon
5.	tintinnabulation	e.	making better or greater, improvement
6.	prevarication	f.	elaboration by the use of exaggerated detail
7.	augmentation	g.	preference for something
8.	predilection	h.	lacking courage, cowardly
9.	embellishment	i.	struck with surprise, astounded
10.	ineffable	j.	the act of evading the truth

B. Fill in the blank with the correct word from Part A.

1. He was _____ that after all he had done for his daughter, she repaid him by eloping with her lover.

2. Once you see through the _____s to his speech, you'll discover he's not sincere in helping the residents at all.

3. What a lovely sound — the _____ from the old church greeting us on Christmas morning.

4. I'm sure she went in for breast _____ treatments — she wasn't so top-heavy the last time I saw her!

5. Michael has a _____ for fast cars and beautiful women.

6. I slept through the entire talk on corporate law — it was all _____ to me — and woke up when they announced the buffet was ready.

7. The movie evoked such _____ sadness that you could actually hear loud sobbing from the audience.

8. Leaving his family behind in the war-torn country was an indescribably _____ act, even for someone as selfish as he was.

9. After a lot of _____, the doctor finally told him that he had probably mere months to live.

10. Discovering that she had a twin sister was indeed _____; the girls had been brought up on two different continents but had ended up taking the same course in the same university.

Now that you've looked at bombastic, grandiloquent, ostentatious words, let's turn our attention to the opposite — short, one- or two-syllable, three-letter words. It's not necessary to use wordy or flowery words to produce a good piece of writing. Often short words, used aptly, will do just as well. Besides, knowing these three-letter words will help you in your next game of Scrabble!

A. Complete the crossword puzzle.

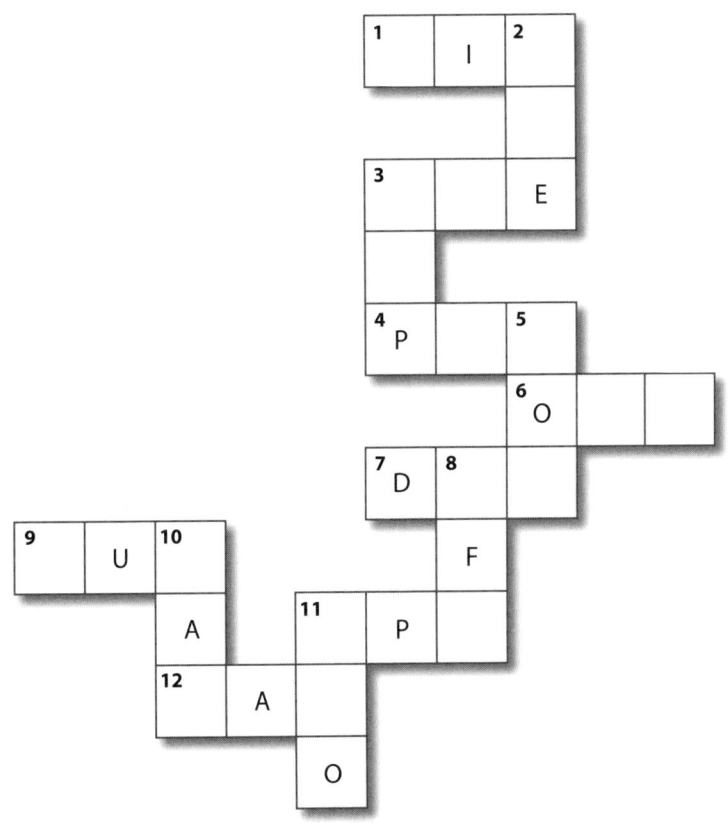

CLUES

1 across: The three of us are going to _____ for a spot in the finals of the singing competition.

2 down: He managed to _____ out a living by working as a labourer in the day and moonlighting as a security guard at night.

3 across: 'I _____ the day that you were born!' exclaimed the poor woman who was ill-treated by her son.

3 down: I was amused by the quote on the sewing kit: 'As you sew, so shall you _____.'

4 across: I wish my parents wouldn't _____ into my private life so much.

5 down: A bunch of _____s wolf-whistled and made rude gestures at me as I crossed the street.

6 across: If things are as bad at work as you say, you can always _____ for early retirement.

7 across: He's a _____ hand at building model planes. You should see his collection — it's really lovely.

8 down: We were told to stow our luggage in the _____ section of the boat.

9 across: Batman and Robin were known as the Dynamic _____.

10 down: He stumbled into the room and sent a whole pile of plates crashing onto the floor — what an _____!

11 across: It would be good if you could start your book with an _____ quotation.

11 down: Without further _____, he introduced the speaker.

12 across: My daughter wants her nose pierced. She says all her friends are doing it — I do hope it's a passing _____!

B. Unscramble the six letters to make two words, then fill them into the blanks.

1. I had to _____ the heavy suitcase up four flights of steps.

2. The young teacher was rather _____ in maintaining class discipline.

U G A L X L

3. We decided to _____ him with the most expensive food in the restaurant to get him to divulge his secret.

4. I can't stand pretty little boy bands and other groups of that _____.

L K Y L I P

5. That was a particularly bad time in his life, when his fortunes were at a low _____.

6. Michelle has a _____ for hot, spicy food — the spicier, the better!

E B N E Y B

7. The boys managed to _____ a makeshift roof using the tarpaulin.

8. The politician tried to _____ the people to vote for him by throwing lavish banquets and promising all kinds of improvements to the estate.

G O I O W R

Vocab List   **Short Words**

aft — towards the back
apt — likely
duo — a pair
ebb — point of decline
fad — style or activity which is popular for a short time
ilk — family or class
lax — not strict
lug — to carry with difficulty
oaf — rude, awkward person
opt — to make a choice from two or more options
ply — to keep giving large quantities of food or drink
pry — to ask questions
rig — to fix in place
rip — to tear
rue — to regret
vie — to compete
woo — to seek the favour of
yen — a craving for
yob — British slang for a hooligan

No Guts, No Glory

One way to learn a new vocabulary word is to write it down a few times as you associate it with the familiar synonymous word.

A. **Here is a list of words synonymous with 'courageous', which is an adjective. In the right-hand column, write the nouns of the words. This exercise is also created to help you see that when you are asked for the meaning of a word, ensure that your answer is in the same part of speech. For example, when prompted for the meaning of 'courage' (noun), write the noun 'bravery', instead of the adjective 'brave', for the answer.**

Adjectives	Nouns
audacious	audacity
bold	
brave	
chivalrous	
daring	
dauntless	
defiant	
doughty	
fearless	
gallant	
gritty	
hardy	
heroic	
indomitable	
intrepid	
invincible	
lion-hearted	
mettlesome	
plucky	
pugnacious	
resolute	
spunky	
stalwart	
stouthearted	
temerarious	
tenacious	
undaunted	
valiant	
venturesome	

B. Sometimes, we may use the names in the box to describe a brave or daring person. Match each of the names with the correct description below. Check out the answers to find out how some of the names came about.

Amazon	David	paladin
Bayard	Don Quixote	Robin Hood
daredevil	Joan of Arc	

1. Like _____, he's chivalrous but impractical.

2. He loves taking dangerous risks. He's such a _____.

3. She's the _____ among us, physically strong and iron-willed.

4. She is the _____ to her platoon for her heroic acts in the war.

5. We fondly called him _____ after he fought off the gigantic bully in school.

6. His fearlessness and courage in the battlefield have made his name synonymous with _____.

7. A _____ of human rights, he called for the immediate release of the student activists.

8. He is the modern-day _____, taking from the rich and giving it to the poor.

Make a boring person stimulating for your reader! Could you describe him as 'insipid'? Perhaps 'nondescript'? What about 'phlegmatic'? And you can do more than render a person as 'interesting'. Is she intriguing? Provocative? Enigmatic?

The words in this unit are all adjectives describing the human condition. We have grouped them in opposite pairs by 'crossing' the words. The more common word in each pair is given for you to find its antonym (a few letters are included as clues). We hope these words will move you to find a characterful of vocabulary to describe the people in your stories.

1.

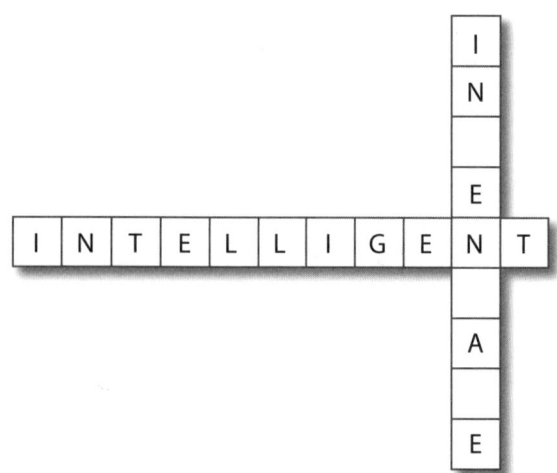

2.

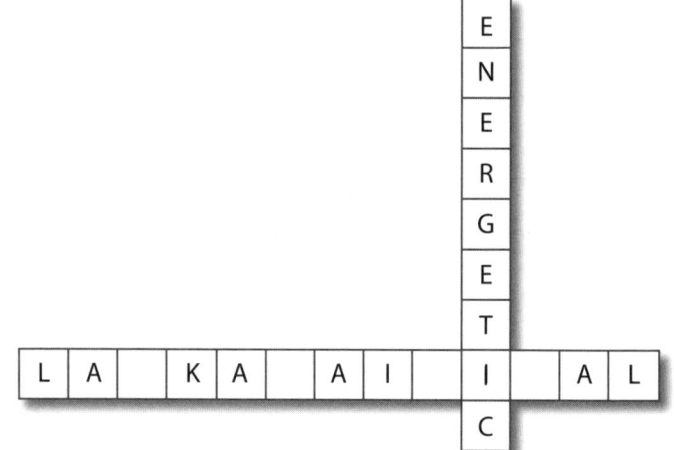

3.

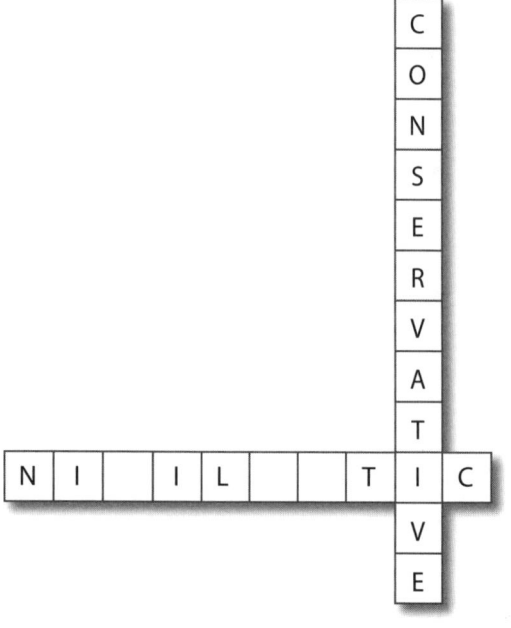

4.

5.

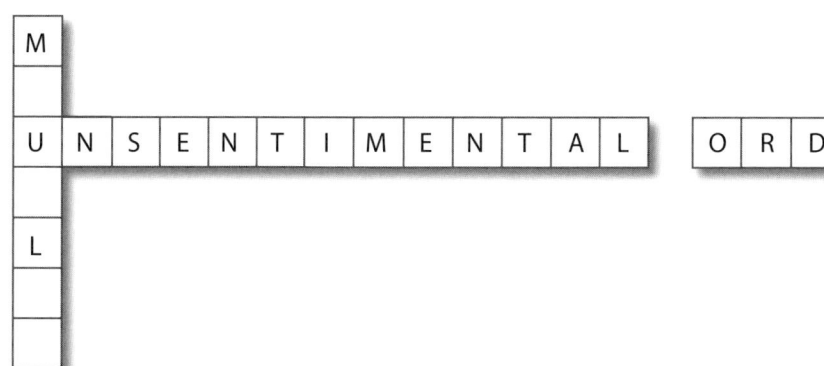

M
U N S E N T I M E N T A L
L

6.

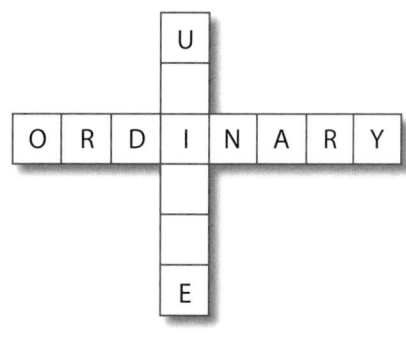

U
O R D I N A R Y
E

7.

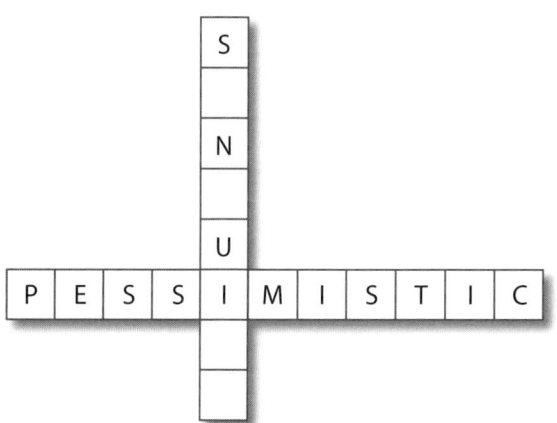

S
N
U
P E S S I M I S T I C

8.

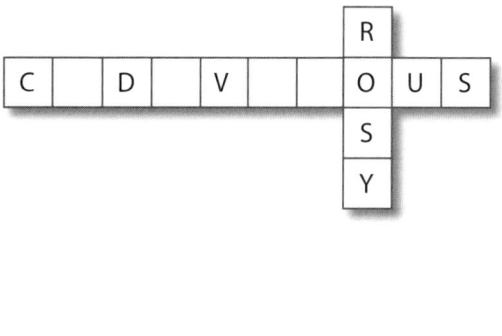

R
C D V O U S
S
Y

9.

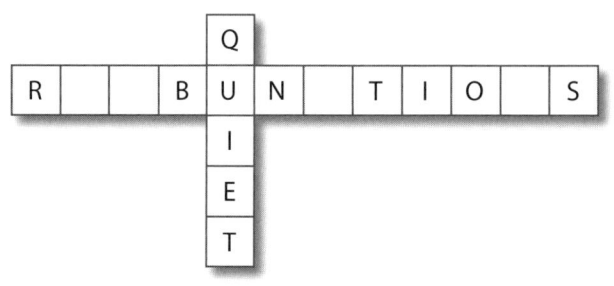

Q
R B U N T I O S
U
I
E
T

10.

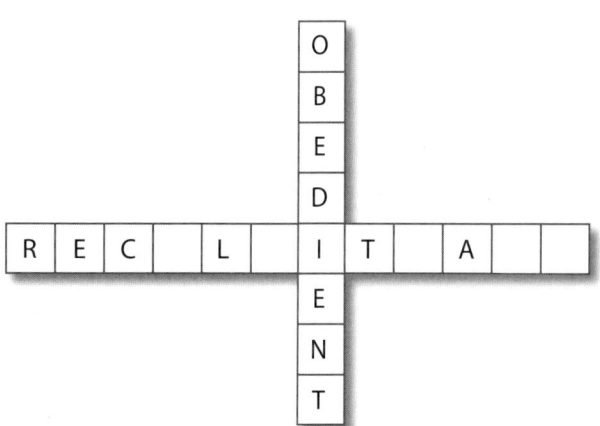

O
B
E
D
R E C L I T A
E
N
T

11.

12.

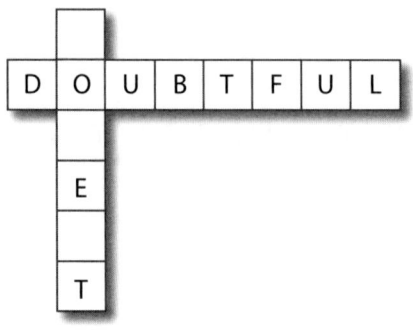

13.

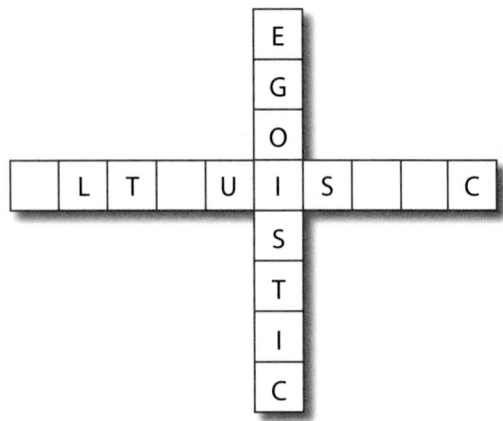

14.

15.

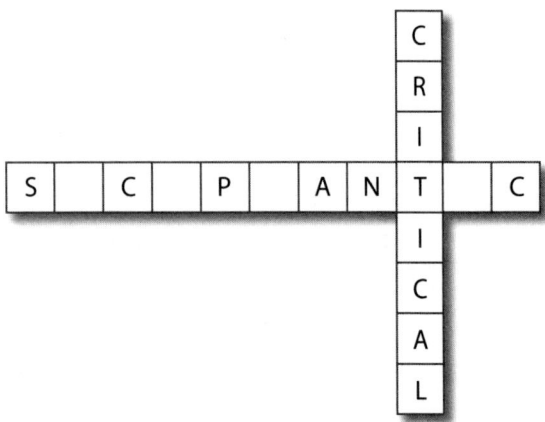

A Pearl Of Great Price

Do you know what *birthstones* are? Birthstones are precious gems that are associated with the different months of the year and are supposed to be lucky if worn by people who are born in those months. There are different birthstone lists but here we use the modern (American) list.

A. Unscramble the letters to form the correct birthstone for the month. The first letter is the correct one.

1.	January	**g** t a e n r	_____
2.	February	**a** y t s h e t m	_____
3.	March	**a** m r q a n i e u a	_____
4.	April	**d** m d a o i n	_____
5.	May	**e** e a d l m r	_____
6.	June	**p** l e r a	_____
7.	July	**r** y u b	_____
8.	August	**p** t i d o e r	_____
9.	September	**s** e i r p a p h	_____
10.	October	**o** l p a	_____
11.	November	**c** t e i i r n	_____
12.	December	**t** s u u i o r q e	_____

B. Fill in each blank with a suitable birthstone from the list above.

1. The model has the perfect face — lovely eyes, straight nose, _____-red lips and _____ly white teeth.

2. I love the colours of the sea — _____, _____ and _____.

3. Don't waste your time advising him on what to do with his life — he simply won't listen. It'll be like casting your _____ before swine.

4. Matthew is a rough _____ — he's intelligent, articulate and personable, but he lacks refinement.

Greek and Roman mythology gives us stories of the exploits of gods and heroes. You may be familiar with some of them — Zeus, Hercules and Hermes, to name a few. These names give rise to words that are associated with the particular qualities of the character in mythology. For example, Hercules was the son of the god Zeus and was renowned for his great strength and courage, so when someone is said to perform a *Herculean* task, it means that the task is difficult to perform, calling for great strength and courage.

A. Do you know who these characters in mythology are? Match the names with the correct identities.

1. Prometheus

2. Tantalus

3. Midas

4. Gorgon

5. Narcissus

6. Mnemosyne

7. Nemesis

8. Pandora

9. Siren

10. Hypnos

a. She opened a forbidden box and let out all the ills of mankind.

b. Goddess of retribution.

c. He stole fire from heaven for the benefit of mankind.

d. A being that sang so enchantingly that she lured sailors to their deaths.

e. He was in love with his own reflection and was turned into a flower.

f. One of three female monsters that had snakes for hair; its appearance was so horrible that one look at it would turn a person to stone.

g. God of sleep.

h. Goddess of memory.

i. He was given the power to turn anything he touched to gold.

j. He was condemned by the gods to hang from the branches of a fruit tree over a pool of water. When he bent to drink, the water would recede and when he reached for a fruit, the wind would blow it away from his reach.

B. Now see if you can fill in the blanks with the words formed from these characters.

1. _____ is a state of consciousness in which a person is apparently asleep but can respond to questions asked by the person who put him or her into this state.

2. Globalisation is a _____; it may seem to provide a wealth of opportunities for some but at the same time it threatens the livelihood of many others.

3. You can remember the colours of the rainbow — violet, indigo, blue, green, yellow, orange, red — by using this _____ to help you: 'V I Boys Get Your Orange Ready!'

4. He was enticed into dabbling in stocks and shares by the _____ prospect of making a lot of money in a very short time.

5. When I paint, I am actually indulging in my _____ tendencies — I love to hear people praise my work!

6. The famous scientist was _____ in spirit and deed; you can always count on him to be creative in his work.

7. That man has the _____; every business venture he has engaged in has prospered.

8. Her lame brother is her _____: he is a constant reminder of the consequences of a moment's folly on her part.

9. The actress was a _____; men were attracted to her in droves.

10. What a _____ that woman is — she's enough to put men off women for life!

An *exhaustive* report is one that is *thorough* — meaning it is complete in every way. It is not to be confused with *exhausting* which means 'tiring out'. A report can also be *searching*, meaning that it is both thorough and *penetrating*, that is, it analyses the subject and gives *cogent* (convincing) reasons in support of the arguments.

A. Unscramble the words in the following sentences — they all have the meaning of things being done very well. Write the words in the blanks provided. Do not move the letters in bold.

1. It is a lew**l**–**d**mtuoence**d** fact that smoking causes lung cancer.

2. The FBI agents carried out an xeaht**s**ie**v**u search of the entire area — they left no stone unturned.

3. The award-winning book provides some eari**c**shn**g** insights into the breakdown of family values today.

4. The student won high praise for the te**g**on**c** arguments he made in the debate.

5. The politician, who has a reputation of being forceful and coming right to the point, gave an **i**cnii**sve** analysis of the problem.

6. My boss is a very temciu**luos** person, and insists on us checking the proofs at least three times before she will approve them.

7. The victim gave a very rc**c**uaat**e** description of the criminal that led to his immediate arrest.

8. The coroner presented his findings in **p**nia**s**ktag**ni** detail, making sure that the listeners understood all the implications of the investigation.

9. The chef was the **c**nso**um**tma**e** master of creating the most delicious desserts.

10. The chief detective won **ue**n**q**ci**v**aulo praise for his handling of the high-profile case.

1. _____
2. _____
3. _____
4. _____
5. _____
6. _____
7. _____
8. _____
9. _____
10. _____

B. Now complete the sentence by filling in the blank with a word which has the opposite meaning to the word in italics. Choose the correct word from the box below.

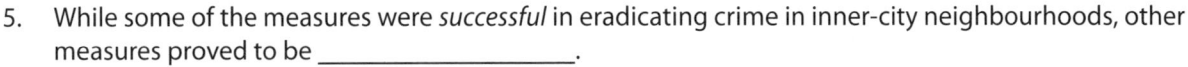

| superficial | lame | sketchy | ineffective | unconvincing |

1. None of the bystanders could give a *detailed* account of the robber's appearance; everyone gave very _____ descriptions.

2. Unlike your brother's *valid* reasons for being late, your excuses are extremely _____.

3. The police did not conduct an *exhaustive* investigation; in fact, they only made _____ enquiries about the incident.

4. You have to present *cogent* arguments if you want to score high marks for your term paper — you certainly won't do that if you give such _____ arguments like these.

5. While some of the measures were *successful* in eradicating crime in inner-city neighbourhoods, other measures proved to be _____.

Vocab List Well And Not Well

accurate — without any mistake
cogent — clearly expressed
consummate — complete in every way
exhaustive — complete
incisive — intelligent and showing understanding of issues
ineffective — not producing the effects that are wanted
lame — not deserving to be believed
meticulous — paying great attention to every detail
painstaking — correct, and using a lot of effort
searching — intended to find the truth about
sketchy — not containing many details
superficial — concerned with the surface, not detailed
unconvincing — not sounding believable
unequivocal — without any doubt, total
well-documented — supported with sufficient facts/evidence

Murder Most Foul

Do you enjoy reading crime fiction or murder mysteries? These are stories that revolve around solving crimes or mysteries. Usually there is a clever detective, lots of clues and suspects, and an unexpected ending.

A. Read the clues and solve the puzzle.

1.							E		B		L			T	
2.				E		E	C			O	N				
3.				P			T	A		O			S		
4.						O		R		R		O			
5.	A		A		E	U									
6.		F		I											
7.				R		N		I							
8.			E	R		E		R		T	O				
9.				M		T		V							
10.					I	B									
11.						U		T							
12.			W		O	D			N						
13.						W		S							

CLUES

1. Ellis Peters wrote about Brother Cadfael, a medieval monk who used his talents as a _____ to solve murders. He had acquired his vast knowledge of the medicinal value of plants when he was a crusader in the Holy Land.

2. It's intriguing to read how the criminal avoids _____ in the course of the story, and it's satisfying to know how he is inevitably found out in the end.

3. In the detective novel I'm reading, the _____, the central character of the story, is also the police inspector who solves the crime.

4. One subcategory of crime fiction is the _____ drama, where the focus is on the law, crime, punishment, and the legal profession.

5. The crime solver in this story is an _____ detective — he loves the challenge of solving crimes and doesn't mind not getting paid for his work.

6. The detective in crime fiction often has a _____, usually an assistant, whose role in the story is to serve as a contrast, thus emphasising the detective's character traits and powers of deduction.

7. Modern-day crime drama focuses a lot on _____ evidence, made possible by scientific advances like DNA fingerprinting.

8. In a typical crime mystery the reader is provided with clues to deduce who the _____ of the crime is. Often, it is the least likely suspect.

9. The prosecutor showed that the defendant's _____ for committing the murder was greed, and it was enough to convince the jury to return a guilty verdict.

10. The suspect provided a watertight _____ — he was at a business seminar when the crime was committed and could be vouched for by any number of colleagues.

11. The term 'inside job' refers to a crime committed by a person in a position of _____ who has access to a key location or has special knowledge.

12. P. D. James and Dorothy L. Sayers were two of the best writers of the _____, which is a complex, plot-driven story in which the reader is provided with clues to guess who did the crime before the answer is revealed at the end of the book.

13. I thoroughly enjoyed every detail of this book — the crime itself, the arrival of the famous investigator, the bungling police, the false suspects, the reconstruction of the crime, and the final, surprising _____ in the plot.

B. The vertical box in the puzzle contains the name of a famous fictional detective. Who is he and who was the writer?

 **Vocab List Crime!**

alibi — proof that someone could not have done what he was accused of
amateur — lacking in skill, doing something for the pleasure of it and not as a job
courtroom — room where a court of law meets
detection — the work of investigating a crime
foil — contrast
forensic — using scientific methods to discover information about a crime
herbalist — someone who grows or sells herbs for medicinal uses
motive — reason for doing something
perpetrator — someone who has committed a crime
protagonist — important character
trust — to have confidence in
twist — unexpected turn
whodunit — story dealing with a crime and its solution

It Takes Two

A *portmanteau* word (or simply, *portmanteau*) is a word formed by blending the sounds and meanings of two different words. The term was first used by Lewis Carroll, the author of *Alice's Adventures in Wonderland*. In the sequel, *Through the Looking Glass*, Carroll coined words like *slithy* (from *slimy* and *lithe*) and chortle (from *chuckle* and *snort*).

A. Combine two words together in the box below to make a legitimate portmanteau.

information	education	advertising	entertainment
exercise	commercial	cafeteria	camera
fact	index	citizen	biography
icon	situation	electronics	editorial
drama	Internet	jazz	lunch
fiction	emotion	fog	dictionary
animation	buffet	breakfast	picture
comedy	documentary	broadcast	cybernetic
smoke	rolling	organism	simultaneous
recorder			

B. Complete the sentences with the portmanteau words taken from the box on page 76. Make sure you use the correct form of the word.

1. The Science Centre is holding an exhibition of dinosaur _____ — the dinosaurs are so realistic it feels like you're in the movie *Jurassic Park*!

2. A new _____ has just opened near the Esplanade. Eat as much as you can for only $15! And for breakfast, lunch and dinner too!

3. Her husband bought a _____ so that they can make home movies of the family when they go on vacation to the Maldives later this year.

4. I think people have a responsibility to contribute to social change by sharing their views online with other _____.

5. The _____ of Leonardo Da Vinci was very well made, I thought. It showed life in Florentine during the 15th and 16th centuries as well as dramatised episodes of Da Vinci's life.

6. I'm going to give a _____ to my colleague so he can organise his collection of name cards.

7. I enjoy _____ more than other forms of aerobic exercise because it incorporates dance routines set to popular music.

8. I love the funny _____ you can download free from this cool website, which I can use to express my feelings and my personality when I chat with others online.

9. I love watching the _____ *Frasier* — it has just the right blend of characters and humorous situations.

10. I was thinking of buying my friend a _____ set for Christmas. It's a fun board game, and my friend is quite good at drawing.

We all have friends who have very unattractive characteristics or personality. But we seldom want to offend them by using unpleasant words to describe them. Well, we can make them a little more charming than they really are by using euphemisms. A euphemism is a polite word or expression you use instead of an unpleasant or offensive one.

Look at the words on the left. Then match each word to its euphemism on the right.

1. a. lazy
   b. moody
   c. ordinary

   banal
   mercurial
   languorous

2. a. disrespectful
   b. sarcastic
   c. meddlesome

   irreverent
   officious
   ironic

3. a. embittered
   b. argumentative
   c. threatening

   litigious
   acrid
   intimidating

4. a. insensitive
   b. reckless
   c. interfering

   intrusive
   stolid
   audacious

5. a. disappointed
   b. empty-headed
   c. narrow-minded

   parochial
   vacuous
   chagrined

6. a. weird
   b. appeasing
   c. flashy

   conciliatory
   unusual
   flamboyant

7. a. mawkish
   b. greedy
   c. prying

   avid
   enquiring
   sentimental

8. a. abnormal
   b. forceful
   c. unexceptional

   dynamic
   uncharacteristic
   tolerable

Unit 37   It's All In The List

Compiling a list of words related to a topic is a useful means of building your vocabulary. Not only that, it is an effective approach to writing an essay. For example, if you are to write a topic about an environmental issue, you can jot down environment-related words to ensure that the content of your essay has key words and substance to carry the essay through.

A. The terms below are all related to the environment. Find and circle all the terms in the word square. The words or phrases run from left to right, right to left, up or down, and diagonally. (Note: Phrases of two words are included in the word square without a space between the words.)

acid rain	contamination	nuclear waste
alternative fuels	ecosystem	overfishing
biodegradable	food chain	ozone depletion
biodiversity	food web	radioactivity
biosphere	global warming	smog
carbon dioxide	greenhouse effect	wildlife
carcinogen	hazardous waste	
conservation	nature reserve	

```
O G Y B E N A B Z H K G S D O N T
Z L T I C I C E M V O X L V A C B
O O I O O A I W S M X G E T E I W
N B V D S H D D S M W R U F O N Z
E A I I Y C R O D S F R F D H O N
D L T V S D A O Q I E E E N N I O
E W C E T O I F S R E G V E U T I
P A A R E O N H E S R T I G C A T
L R O S M F I S U A S H T O L V A
E M I I J N E O D O O O A N E R N
T I D T G R H A Y X T N N I A E I
I N A Y V N B S Q R N V R C R S M
O G R E E L B D D C H W E R W N A
N E F E E F I L D L I W T A A O T
C R R B I O S P H E R E L C S C N
U G H A Z A R D O U S W A S T E O
E D I X O I D N O B R A C T E G C
```

B. Now, in the space below compile a list of words you may use to write on a topic about stress (or some other topic of interest).

Unit 38 — What A Poltroon Would Say Of Himself …

In Unit 29, you learnt some synonyms of 'courageous'. In this unit, you will encounter some words which are synonyms of its opposite: 'timid'.

Complete the words in the puzzle and see how many of these words you know. There are 20 words altogether. By the way, do you know what a 'poltroon' in the unit title is?

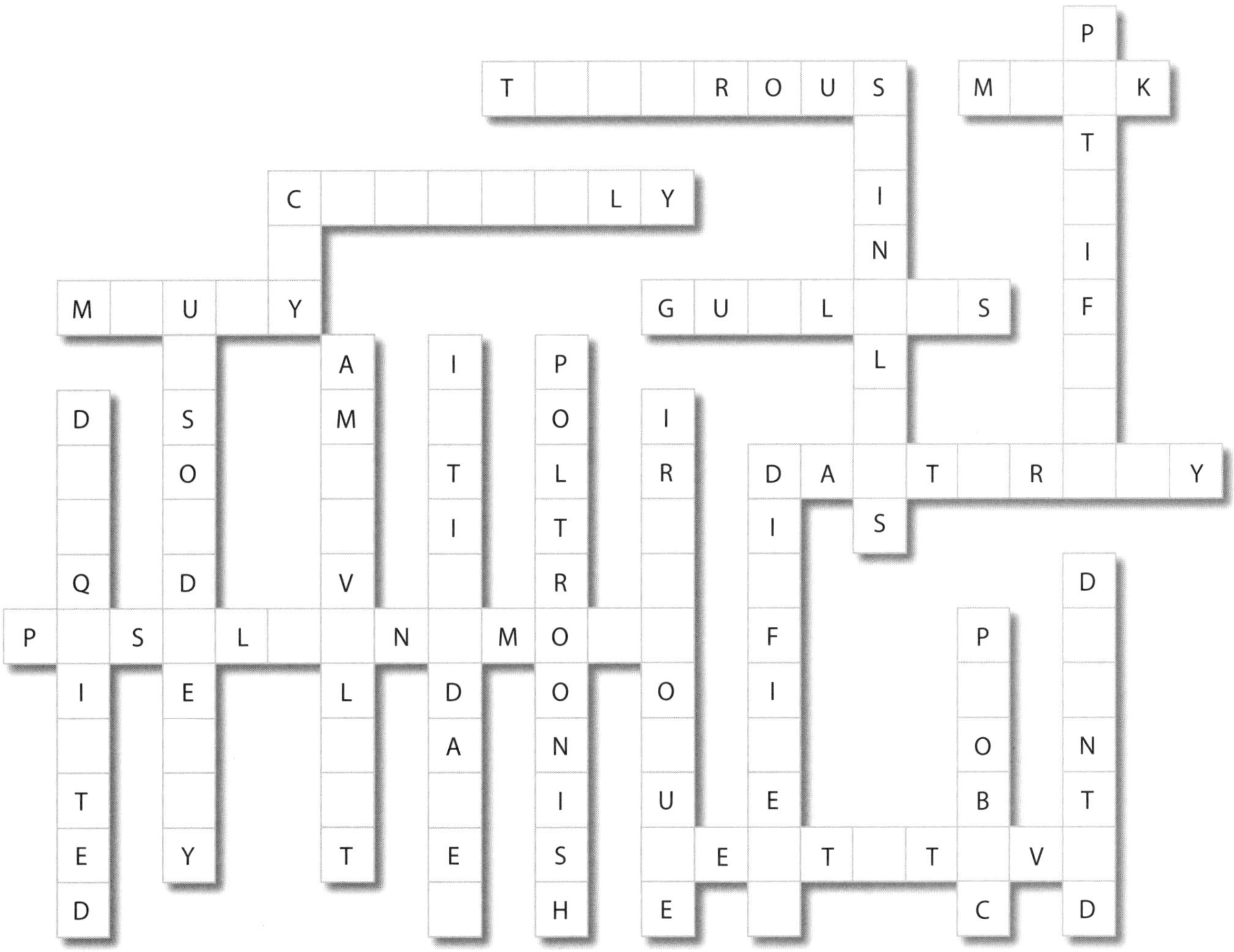

Complete the word ladder using the clues provided on the next page. The words contain the meaning 'beauty'. What word is formed by the central spine of the ladder and what does it mean?

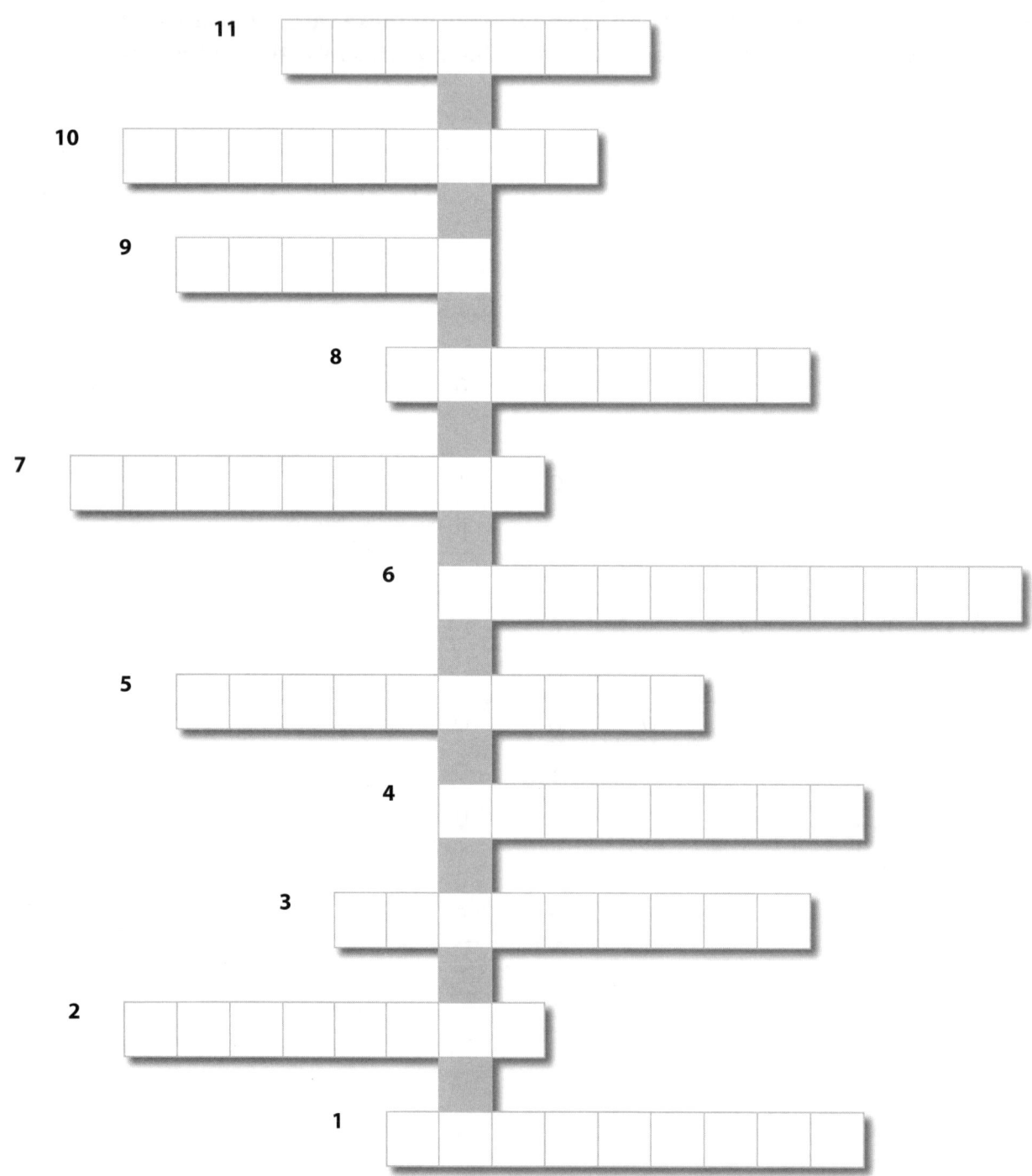

CLUES

1 building with little _____ appeal
2 woman with drop-dead _____ eyes
3 _____ little pearl
4 _____ dress with sapphire sequins
5 _____ Ming vase
6 _____ peacock feathers
7 _____ occasion attended by celebrities
8 girl with _____ features
9 _____ view of the hills
10 _____ red-head with great looks
11 girl with _____ legs

 **Beautiful!**

aesthetic — having great beauty
alluring — very attractive, seductive
comely — pleasing in appearance
exquisite — very beautiful, delicate
glamorous — attractive in an exciting way
gorgeous — splendid in appearance
ornamental — beautiful rather than useful
pulchritudinous — physically beautiful
ravishing — very attractive
resplendent — having a splendid appearance
scenic — having beautiful scenery
seemly — pleasing in appearance
shapely — having a pleasing shape (used for a woman's figure)
striking — attracting attention by being easily noticed
stunning — extremely beautiful or attractive

Now Tell It Like It Is

In Unit 36, we learnt a few euphemisms, words used to avoid offending someone. In this unit, let's do the opposite, that is, find words which convey an impertinent attitude in place of inoffensive or less unpleasant words.

Rewrite the following sentences by replacing the italicised expressions containing euphemistic language with more simple, direct words or phrases which form dysphemisms — harsher substitutes for 'gentler' terms. An example has been done for you.

1. She's *not the best cook in the world*.

    She's a terrible cook.

2. He *wasn't entirely truthful*.

3. He *could have been more careful*.

4. He's *chubby and advanced in years*.

5. We had to have our Labrador *put to sleep*.

6. In the middle of the test I had to *answer a call of nature*.

7. You were *rather merry* last evening after three cans of beer.

8. Your product is *not up to standard*.

9. There are many people who are *financially challenged* and need *active employment* in the country.

_____

10. The tour guide advised us to avoid the *less salubrious* parts of the town.

_____

11. You've *displayed a blatant disregard of others' feelings*.

_____

12. The discussions have *not been fruitful*.

_____

13. His coat *had seen better days*.

_____

14. The old man *passed away* last night.

_____

15. *Senior citizens* need not pay the entrance fees to the zoo.

_____

16. He's *between jobs*.

_____

17. The supervisor *laid him off* because he was *unmotivated*.

_____

18. The lieutenant could not explain the *collateral damage* caused by the military action.

_____

19. There are many *less privileged members of the society* who need our help.

_____

20. After a series of *deferred success*, she's beginning to doubt herself.

_____

Unit 41   **Ahead Of The Pack**

If you overhear someone making a remark that 'she's a bridesmaid, never a bride', do you know what this means? Or if someone accuses you of being a flash in the pan, is he or she being complimentary? There are many idiomatic expressions that can be used to describe people. Let's see whether you're ahead of the pack in doing this exercise!

Read the descriptions and write the correct idioms in the blanks. Choose from the idioms in the box on page 89. You do not have to use up all the idioms.

1. She tried her best to make the pouch in craft class, but she doesn't seem to be good with her hands.

   She's

   _____

2. I was really surprised to find that Elaine is head of human resources — she's the most aloof and unfriendly person I've known. She actually scowled at me when I was introduced to her on my first day!

   She's

   _____

3. Martin is just like his father — easy-going, charming, hates to see anyone unhappy, especially the ladies.

   He's

   _____

4. Some buddy Su Chen turned out to be — at the first hint of trouble, she left me to face the music by myself.

   She's

   _____

5. But I just told you how to access the data half an hour ago!

You've _____

6. That cute singer may be popular now, but give it a year or so, and no one will remember her.

She's _____

7. I can't believe we hired that young graduate. He doesn't seem to know anything!

He's _____

8. He's the most influential news publisher in the past decade.

He's _____

9. I liked Lynn the moment I met her. We had a lot in common — the same tastes in books and music, the same outlook in life.

She's _____

10. I don't think you can trust her ideas — she's terribly impractical at the best of times.

She's got her _____

11. Lyndy is just the opposite — she's the most practical person I've ever met.

She's got her

_____

12. I don't think you'll be able to persuade your boss to give you a raise — he's not one to give way easily.

He's

_____

13. I do believe that Marcus hasn't been sick a day in his life!

He has the

_____

14. She's a very shy girl. She'd shrivel up whenever you talk to her.

She's

_____

a man's man	a fairweather friend	a shrinking violet
an eager beaver	a hard nut to crack	a kindred spirit
fish out of water	wet behind the ears	a chip off the old block
feet on the ground	a babe in the woods	head in the clouds
a cold fish	a mover and shaker	a closed book
quick off the mark	all fingers and thumbs	a memory like a sieve
a flash in the pan	ahead of the pack	a barrel of laughs
constitution of an ox		

A piece of writing that is concise and to the point is a joy to read. For example, which sentence sounds better: 'The movie critic adopted *with complete lack of originality* the opinions of other writers' or 'The movie critic adopted the opinions of other writers *slavishly*'? Being able to pick a suitable word to do the job of several words is also a valuable skill to put into practice when you are writing a summary.

Replace each group of words in italics with a suitable adjective, and rewrite the new sentence in the space provided. All the adjectives end in the suffix '-ous'.

1. It is easier to teach a class *that is fairly consistent in having students of the same level*.

    _____

2. When you write an essay for the exam, make sure that you do not introduce material *that is not directly relevant to the topic*.

    _____

3. Her vivacity and high spirits are *likely to spread to or influence others and make them feel the same way*.

    _____

4. The boys are especially *merry* today, *but in a noisy way*.

    _____

5. Rock climbing in this part of the world can be dangerous because of the *unpredictable and ever-changing* weather.

    _____

6. I can't stand that man because he is *intrusive and always offers advice that is unwanted*.

    _____

7. I know the sea looks peaceful and calm now, but it can *turn on you when you least expect it*.

    _____

8. The audience broke into *natural and unforced* applause as the dance came to an end.

    _____

9. I've always thought that it must be a useful skill to have — *being able to use both left and right hand with equal ease.*

_____

10. The dress that Cheryl wore at the prom was *shocking and beyond all reasonable limits* — I'm surprised her mother allowed her to wear it!

_____

11. The taxi driver intentionally took a more *roundabout and indirect* route.

_____

12. Several cracks *that had a threatening aspect* began to appear in the wall.

_____

13. I'm sure you will find her an excellent employee: hardworking and *careful to do what is right.*

_____

14. I found the views written in the editorial *capable of more than one interpretation.*

_____

 **Words Ending With '-ous'**

ambidextrous — able to use both hands equally well
ambiguous — having more than one possible meaning
boisterous — energetic
cantankerous — bad-tempered, tending to argue a lot
capricious — changeable, unpredictable
circuitous — not straight or direct
conscientious — hardworking and dedicated
extraneous — not directly connected to
homogeneous — consisting of parts which are similar to one another
infectious — affecting many
mellifluous — sounding pleasant and flowing
melodious — pleasing to listen to
officious — having too high an opinion of one's importance
ominous — indicating something unpleasant is likely to happen
outrageous — shocking and morally unacceptable
spontaneous — happening in a natural, often sudden way
superfluous — more than is needed or wanted
tortuous — not direct or simple
treacherous — dangerous

Here's To Your Health

Do you feel hale and hearty, and full of beans? Or do you feel off-colour and slightly flu-ish? Do you know what a coronary thrombosis is? When someone suffers from hypertension, what does it mean? This exercise is all about healthy and sick words. The next time you visit your doctor, you don't have to be intimidated by him or her spouting medical jargon at you.

A. The box below contains words and idiomatic expressions that describe the healthy and the sick. Put the words under the correct heading.

ailing	athletic	delicate
infirm	robust	malnourished
vigorous	at death's door	a clean bill of health
wan	in the pink	virile
in rude health	strapping	feeble
go under the knife	debilitated	bedridden
blooming	emaciated	hardy
under the weather	flourishing	indisposed

Healthy	Sick

B. Fill in the blank with the correct word. You can choose from the words in the box.

panacea	apoplexy
contagion	inflammation
hypochondriac	haemorrhage
hypertension	coronary
congenital	relapse

1. During the outbreak of SARS, patients were isolated in special wards so that there would be no risk of _____.

2. After the operation, she was on the mend, but inexplicably she had a _____ and went into a coma.

3. My mother's being treated for _____; she has to take pills every day to control her blood pressure.

4. The accident victim suffered from massive internal bleeding and eventually died of a brain _____.

5. Mankind has always dreamt of a remedy for all diseases or a _____.

6. There's actually nothing physically wrong with him, but his preoccupation with his health is turning him into a _____.

7. The doctor told Mike that if he didn't control his diet, have more exercise and continue taking his blood pressure pills, there was a high chance he would suffer a stroke or _____.

8. A _____ disease is one that is inherited or transmitted genetically from parent to child.

9. The doctor noted the symptoms — swelling, redness, irritation — and told him he had severe _____ of the eye.

10. _____ thrombosis is the obstruction of blood flow in an artery by a blood clot and can lead to a heart attack or stroke.

Words can sometimes have positive or negative connotations which refer to the associations or ideas implied by a word. For example, Wall Street holds connotations of great wealth and power.

Each person below has his or her own opinions about someone. Fill in the blanks with the correct words from the box below. These words can have either positive or negative connotations.

glib	permissive	trusting	frank
meticulous	broad-minded	articulate	imaginative
obsequious	insincere	lackadaisical	helpful
keen	anti-social	self-reliant	fanatical
fussy	officious	tactful	laid-back
gullible	blunt	respectful	fanciful

1.

It's a good thing to be _____ to your elders.

But my brother is being _____ to our rich uncle in the hope of inheriting his wealth.

2.

Sam has always been a hit with women, being charming and _____.

But lately I feel he has become too _____ in his manner.

3.

It's easy to pull off an April Fool's joke on Soon Hock — he's a _____ soul.

But he's too _____ if you ask me.

4.

I think you should give that project to Jessie — she's very _____, and can be counted on to do a good job.

Yes, but to the point of being _____ and uncooperative — she's simply not a team player.

5.

Now don't start her on the subject of rock climbing, or we'll be listening to her for hours.

I know; she's past being _____ on it — she's absolutely _____ about it!

6.

I think I'm fairly _____ on the subject of teenagers having an active social life.

Yes, but Lisa's parents are too _____ — they let her stay out late even on weeknights.

7.

A good editor must be _____ about her work.

I agree, but at the same time she has to know when not to be overly _____, especially when there are pressing deadlines.

8.

The bosses seem to like Casper's work — they say it's highly _____.

But I personally think some of his ideas are way out there — just too _____!

9.

I think Candice should learn to curb her tongue — she's too _____.

Well, I think she's refreshingly _____.

10.

How _____ of that sales lady to say I looked good in this outfit — it's obvious that I didn't!

I think she was just trying to be _____ — she said you'd look good if you took a little weight off.

11.

Don't be angry with Seet — he was just trying to be _____ when he offered his advice.

Well, I think he was being _____ — I never asked his advice!

12.

You have to admire his _____ attitude — not many people can enjoy a game of golf before an important presentation the next day.

You think so? Well, I think he's just plain _____!

Comings And Goings

There is a lot going on in the world, as the following words in the left-hand column will tell you. Each of the words is related to a happening or event. Keep track of the world's comings and goings by committing these words and their meanings to memory!

A. Match each word to the correct definition in the right-hand column.

1.	boycott	a.	a sudden and sometimes violent attempt by the citizens or army to take control of the government
2.	brigandage	b.	a refusal by a group to buy or use something as a show of protest
3.	carnage	c.	a violent upheaval, such as that caused by an earthquake, which causes great destruction
4.	cataclysm	d.	the massive killing and wounding of people, especially in a war
5.	contretemps	e.	a government ban on trade with a foreign country
6.	coup	f.	the dispersion of a people from their original homeland
7.	diaspora	g.	robbery and plundering committed by armed bands, often taking place in mountainous regions
8.	embargo	h.	an inopportune or embarrassing situation
9.	exigency	i.	a source of widespread dreadful devastation caused by a deadly disease or war
10.	fete	j.	a pressing or urgent situation which requires immediate attention
11.	fiasco	k.	a totally destructive event, for example, a nuclear catastrophe, which causes massive death toll
12.	fluke	l.	an elaborate outdoor party
13.	foray	m.	a very dangerous situation involving overheating of a nuclear reactor core, resulting in melting of the core and release of radiation
14.	holocaust	n.	the removal of people, for example, from a political party, whom one considers undesirable, often by violence
15.	meltdown	o.	a total failure, in a way which is embarrassing
16.	purge	p.	a stroke of good luck
17.	scourge	q.	a first attempt into an area which is outside one's expertise

B. The following words are related to war and conflict. Match each word to the correct definition in the right-hand column.

1. ambush

2. belligerency

3. blitz

4. deployment

5. genocide

6. harassment

7. incursion

8. insurgency

9. massacre

10. offensive

11. ouster

12. revolution

13. skirmish

a. an aggressive invasion into foreign territory

b. repeated attacks or raids

c. a revolt by a relatively small group against a recognised government

d. a military attack involving large forces over a long period

e. a sudden, heavy aerial bombardment

f. the indiscriminate killing of a large number of humans, especially those who cannot defend themselves

g. overthrow of one government and its replacement with another

h. warlike conflict which international laws recognise as having legitimate status

i. the strategic distribution of forces in preparation for war

j. the removal of someone from a position of authority

k. a fight between small forces, especially one which happens away from the main battle site

l. the systematic and deliberate killing of a whole group or race of people

m. a sudden attack made from a concealed position

Engage your olfactory sense and smell your way to a successful descriptive essay by throwing an ambrosial feast of words for the reader to partake in! Nose out the following words in bold, and use them as often as you can in your writing. For a start, tickle your olfactory sense by continuing the list of nouns which may be described by the words in bold.

1. **smelly** *socks, toilets,* _____

2. a **foul-smelling** *carcass,* _____

3. the **malodorous** *garbage,* _____

4. the **dank** *cellar,* _____

5. the **pungent** *rotten eggs,* _____

6. the **musty** *drawers,* _____

7. the **noisome** *slums,* _____

8. the **fetid** *muddy water,* _____

9. the **musty** *sofa,* _____

10. the **acrid** *smoke,* _____

11. the **putrid** *flesh of a decayed cat,* _____

12. the **musky** *whiff of cigarette smoke,* _____

13. **fusty** *old winter clothes,* _____

14. a **frowzy** *old cupboard,* _____

15. **stinking** *chamber pots,* _____

16. a **perfumed** *letter,* _____

17. **aromatic** *herbs,* _____

18. **musky** *cologne,* _____

19. **balmy** *body oil,* _____

20. **fruity** *body spray,* _____

21. **spicy** *breath,* _____

22. **odoriferous** *spices,* _____

23. **fresh odorous** *bedsheets,* _____

24. **scented** *candles,* _____

25. **jasmine-scented** *soap,* _____

26. **peppery-scented** *sweat,* _____

27. a **sweet-scented** *morning,* _____

28. the **heady scent** of *wine and perfume,* _____

29. the **smell** of *laundered shirts,* _____

30. the **fragrance** of *white lilies,* _____

31. the **odour** of *clinical rooms,* _____

32. the **scent** of *pine needles,* _____

33. the **stench** of *burning rubber,* _____

34. the **aroma** of *coffee,* _____

35. the **bouquet** of a *fine wine,* _____

36. the **foetor** of *sewage pipes,* _____

37. the **malodour** of *diesel fumes,* _____

38. the **reek** of *stale sweat,* _____

39. the **stink** of *decayed flesh,* _____

40. the **salty tang** of the *ocean air,* _____

41. the **ambrosial smells** of a *chef's kitchen,* _____

42. a *garden* **redolent** of *roses,* a *living room* **redolent** of *floor wax,* _____

Visions Of The Future

Science fiction explores the wonders of the future and tries to answer the question 'what if?'. What if there is intelligent life on other planets? What if we could build intelligent machines? Science fiction (or sci-fi) also warns of potential dangers — what if the world becomes so polluted that it can no longer sustain life? Some well-known sci-fi writers include Isaac Asimov, Ray Bradbury and Arthur C. Clarke.

See if you know some of these terms commonly found in science fiction. Read the clues on the left and fill in the blanks with the correct letters to form the words.

1. A mechanical device that can perform physical tasks. The word was first used by Czech writer Karel Capek in his play *R.U.R.*

   __ o __ o __

2. The branch of engineering that involves the design and manufacture of the mechanical devices in (1) above. This word was first used in print by Isaac Asimov.

   r __ b __ t __ __ s

3. The simulation of human intelligence by computer systems. The short form of this term is A.I.

   a __ t __ __ i __ i __ __ __ i __ __ e __ __ i __ e __ c __

4. A mechanical being that closely resembles a human being in appearance.

   __ n __ __ oi __

5. A being that is composed of both organic and mechanical parts.

   __ y __ o __ g

6. The technology of building devices from single atoms and molecules.

   __ __ n __ t __ ch __ __ l __ g __

7. A virtual reality world that exists inside computers and on computer networks, first coined by the sci-fi writer William Gibson.

   __ y __ e __ s __ __ c __

8. The process of moving objects from one place to another instantaneously.

   t __ l __ __ o __ t __ t __ o __

9. The production of multiple identical copies of an organism.

   __ l __ n __ __ g

10. The process of changing a planet to create a more habitable atmosphere.

    t __ r __ af __ r __ i __ __

11. Originating from outside the earth or its atmosphere.

    __ x __ __ a __ er __ __ s __ __ ia __

12. The process of freezing the human body of a deceased person in the hope of reviving that person when a new cure is found in the future.

    c __ y __ n __ __ s

13. An imagined alternate reality based on the theory that there are other universes that might exist where history is different, for example, John F. Kennedy was not assassinated.

__ a __ __ l __ e __ universe

14. A common plot device in science fiction where time runs normally for a period and then skips back, with most of the characters in the story not being aware of what has happened, that is, they have no recollection of events being repeated.

time l __ __ p

15. The concept of moving backwards and forwards in time, just as we can through space.

time __ r __ __ e __

16. A hypothetical feature of the space-time continuum that acts like a short cut — it would potentially make Question 15 above possible.

w __ r __ h __ __ e

TLAs With TLC*

It is common for people to shorten words and phrases in their speech, especially if they are extra-long names. For example, you would seldom say 'I'll be driving on the Pan-Island Expressway' — you'll just say 'I'll be driving on the PIE'.

There are many types of shortened forms (or *contractions*) in English. They are called *abbreviations* when the words, made up of the initial letters, are read as individual letters — for example, WTO (World Trade Organisation) and BBC (British Broadcasting Corporation). When abbreviations are read as words, we call them *acronyms* — for example, AIDS (Acquired Immune Deficiency Syndrome). If you wonder why some abbreviations do not seem to have been formed from their initial letters, that's because the original words were originally in a foreign language like Latin or French. For example, *etc.* is the shortened form of *et cetera* (a Latin phrase) and means 'and so on'. Yet other forms of abbreviations are pronounced as the full word. For example, *Mr* is pronounced *Mister*. Some are just truncated words, for example, *lab* for *laboratory*. Abbreviations and acronyms are used in writing to save time and avoid clumsy repetition.

A. **Now let's test your knowledge of abbreviations and acronyms. Write the long forms of these abbreviations or acronyms. Write 'ab' for abbreviation and 'ac' for acronym beside each.**

1. IBM
2. scuba**
3. HTML
4. POW
5. LASIK
6. UNICEF
7. ASEAN
8. SMS
9. SARS
10. CNN

* Do you know what TLA and TLC stand for?
** Some acronyms have become so recognisable as common words that they are no longer written in capital letters.

B. Read the following message and write in full what the writer is saying.

From: Sally Sim <simhk@singnet.com.sg>

Sent: Tuesday, September 22, 2006, 10:30 AM

To: <all in mailing list>

Subject: Important Memo — Please Read

Memo to all PMs

Please remind your team members that they are not to engage in MLM activities. The CEO, Mr Sim, has noticed some employees selling tupperware and beauty products during office hours, and has issued a stern statement that everyone is to cease this activity asap. NB: Just because Mr Sim's wife comes in once in a while to sell such products doesn't mean that employees can too.

Regards
Sally Sim
HR Manager

C. Write the texts on the left in full and match them with where they would be found on the right.

1. Absolutely no GM products sold here

2. Dep Singapore 0800 Arr Brisbane 1600

3. *When Death Comes Knocking* (PG) 12 midnight

4. Some FAQs on cholesterol screening

a. health brochure

b. cinema listing

c. airline ticket

d. advertisement in a store selling organic produce

Think

Then there are some curious words that are formed when the initial letters are spelt out. For example, do you know what these words mean: *deejay*, *veejay* and *emcee*?

Unit 49 Face Off

A. Here are some words describing different parts of the face. See if you can tell which part is being described.

double	cauliflower	bloodshot	knitted
pencil-thin	lined	piercing	pierced
flyaway	hollow	receding	hooded
mousy	upturned	sallow	aquiline
pursed	furrowed	full	cleft

eyes — _____

ears — _____

nose — _____

hair — _____

forehead — _____

eyebrows — _____

chin — _____

cheeks — _____

lips — _____

B. Many idiomatic expressions have parts of the face in them. For example, when you *thumb your nose at* someone, it means you do not respect that person. (This expression originated from the actual gesture of putting the thumb to the nose as a rude sign!) Fill in each blank with a suitable idiom with the help of the word in brackets.

1. _____ (mouth) as I watched the fireman try to reach the child on the roof of the building.

2. Her uncharacteristically rude answer caused _____ (eyebrows) in the class.

3. You mustn't resign from your new position just because you are angry at your boss — don't _____ (nose).

4. We've had _____ (ear) for the last month so that we'll be the first to know if the company is going to be sold.

5. Try not to be intimidated by your new job and your new colleagues — keep _____ (chin)!

6. Remember to _____ (hair) when you work with Wally — he'll do his best to rile you and make you lose your cool.

7. The disappointing news that she had failed to enter the university of her choice was a _____ (teeth).

8. When I blurted out at the meeting that it was Steve's fault we couldn't make the deadline, he gave me _____ (eye).

9. The poor lived _____ (cheek) in run-down tenements on the edge of the city — it's no wonder the epidemic spread so fast there.

10. 'Don't _____ (lip), young miss!' hissed the librarian when I tried to explain why the books had come crashing down from the shelf.

Unit 50 Music To My Ears

All of us have our favourite music and musicians. Long before *American Idol* came on the scene, there were many enjoyable musical programmes on television. And nothing quite compares to attending a live musical performance, be it a musical, a classical performance or a rock concert. This exercise is all about music — let's find out how much you know!

A. Circle the word that doesn't belong to the group.

1.   carol   psalm   madrigal   hymn
2.   violin   bassoon   double bass   cello
3.   tuba   trombone   French horn   harp
4.   oboe   viola   piccolo   flute
5.   clarinet   tambourine   bongo   kettledrum
6.   jukebox   gramophone   harpsichord   CD player
7.   soprano   nocturne   sonata   serenade
8.   contralto   tenor   quartet   bass
9.   vocalist   pianist   flautist   violinist
10. rock   hip-hop   ballad   jazz
11. forte   pianissimo   crescendo   alto
12. Mozart   Picasso   Bach   Beethoven

B. Fill in the missing letters to form the correct words.

1.   An _____ consists of a group of musicians who play on instruments that fall into four families — strings, brass, woodwinds and percussion.

	r		h		t		

2.   The place directly in front of and below the stage of a theatre where the musicians perform is called the _____.

		t

3.   A music _____ is a category of music that shares a particular style.

	e		r	

4.   A combination of musical sounds pleasing to the ear is known as _____.

	a		m		n	

5. _____ are a pair of shells of wood or plastic fastened to the thumb and clicked to produce a rhythmic sound.

		s			n	e		

6. A _____ is an instrument that generates sound electronically from stored samples of musical instruments.

	y		t			s				r

7. A guitar player uses a triangle-shaped object called a _____ to strum the guitar.

p			c			u	

8. A _____ is a wind instrument where the player blows air into a bag.

b			p			

Unit **51** What's In A Name? (1)

Some English words owe their existence to the names of persons famous for their contributions to different fields. For example, the Braille system of raised dots that enable a blind person to read was named for its inventor, Louis Braille (1809–1852), a French educator who was blind from the age of three. Samuel Morse gave the world the Morse code, the code used for transmitting messages over the electric telegraph using a sequence of dots and dashes.

Do you know what words these people lent their names to? Write the missing letters in the blanks.

1. Leo Baekeland was a Belgian-born American chemist who invented a hard, durable, black plastic. This plastic is called _____.

B			e			t	e

2. Ambrose Burnside, a Union army general in the American Civil War, was known for a style of men's facial hair. His name gave us the word _____, which are growths of hair down the side of a man's face to below the ears, worn with an unbearded chin.

	i		e		u			s

3. When you refer to a law as being _____, it means that it is unusually harsh or cruel. Draco was a 17th century statesman in Athens who was known for the severity of his sentences for breaking the law — death for almost every offence!

d			c			i		

4. An _____ is a person with refined tastes, especially in food and wine. The word is named after Epicurus, a Greek philosopher who taught that pleasure was the highest good.

	p		c			

5. Thomas Bowdler (1754–1825), an English physician who published a ten-volume edition of the works of Shakespeare in which he omitted words that 'cannot with propriety be read aloud in a family', gave his name to the verb _____, which means to remove parts of a piece of writing that is considered vulgar or offensive.

		w				r			e	

6. When you describe something as being _____, it means that it is ostentatiously smart or fancy. The word gets its name from Cesar Ritz, a Swiss hotelier whose hotels became synonymous with wealth and luxury.

r			z		

7. A _____ is a British policeman, named after Sir Robert Peel (1788–1850), an English statesman who organised the London police force.

	o		b	

8. The _____ are freelance photographers who pursue celebrities to take pictures of them for their magazines or newspapers. The word is named for Paparazzo, a character in the Italian film *La Dolce Vita* (*The Sweet Life*).

p		p			a		z	

9. This is a dessert made with cooked peach halves on vanilla ice cream flavoured with raspberry sauce, created in London to honour the famous Australian soprano Dame Nellie Melba.

P		a				M				a	

10. The _____ _____ is an energetic jitterbug dance. It originated in New York's Harlem during the Great Depression and was very popular. It was named for no apparent reason after Charles Lindbergh, nicknamed Lucky Lindy, who flew solo across the Atlantic in his monoplane, *The Spirit of St Louis*.

L		n						p	

11. If a person is described as being _____ _____, it means he or she is wishy-washy or weakly sentimental. This was actually a nickname given to the English poet Ambrose Philips by his rival Henry Carey who used it in a poem.

n		m				p		m		

12. The word _____ is related to the works of George Orwell, and especially *1984*, his novel describing a future totalitarian state.

O		w				i		

What's In A Name? (2)

Here is another exercise with words derived from names of famous (and infamous!) people.

Match the word with its meaning.

	WORD	NAMED FOR		MEANING
1.	Casanova	Giacomo Casanova (1725–1798), an Italian adventurer	a.	an insolent or impudent person
2.	Peter Principle	Laurence Johnson Peter, a Canadian author who wrote a book called *The Peter Principle* in 1969	b.	an amusement ride made up of a large rotating wheel with suspended seats
3.	quisling	Vidkun Quisling, a Norwegian diplomat who collaborated with the Nazis.	c.	a bath with underwater jets to produce a whirlpool effect to massage the body
4.	sandwich	John Montagu, Earl of Sandwich, an English politician with a passion for gambling	d.	a type of firework that spins round and round as it burns
5.	zeppelin	Count Ferdinand von Zeppelin, a German army officer	e.	a makeshift bomb made of an inflammable liquid and a wick in a glass bottle
6.	Parkinson's Law	Cyril Northcote Parkinson, an English historian and journalist who wrote a book called *Parkinson's Law: The Pursuit of Progress* in 1958.	f.	an inflatable life jacket
7.	leotard	Jules Leotard, a French trapeze artist	g.	a traitor who serves as the puppet of the enemy occupying his country
8.	jackanapes	Jack Napes, nickname of William de la Pole, Duke of Suffolk	h.	a man with a reputation for having love affairs with many women
9.	Ferris wheel	George Ferris, who designed the first wheel in 1892	i.	two or more slices of bread with a filling of meat, egg, vegetables, etc., in between
10.	Catherine wheel	Saint Catherine of Alexandria who was martyred for her defence of Christianity	j.	a raincoat made of rubberised fabric
11.	Mae West	Mae West, a Hollywood movie actress whose ample bust suggested the name for the object	k.	'Work expands so as to fill the time for its completion.'

12.	Jacuzzi	Candido Jacuzzi, an American engineer	l. a cigar-shaped, propeller-driven airship
13.	Molotov cocktail	Vyacheslav Molotov, a Soviet politician	m. the manipulation of electoral district boundaries to give one party a greater advantage
14.	maverick	Samuel Augustus Maverick, a Texas cattle rancher	n. 'In a hierarchy every employee tends to rise to his level of incompetence.'
15.	gerrymander	Elbridge Gerry, a governor of Massachusetts	o. a skin-tight one-piece garment
16.	mackintosh	Charles Macintosh, a Scottish chemist	p. a dissenter, someone who holds unorthodox views

There are many English words that have been borrowed from other languages. For example, 'fjord' and 'slalom' are of Finnish origin (that is, they come from Finland) and 'kayak' and 'igloo' are Eskimo words.

A. Do you know which countries these English words originated from? Put them under the correct country — there are eight words per country.

bistro	cuisine	pasta	vendetta	chauffeur
honcho	delicatessen	sputnik	fiasco	billet-doux
campanile	origami	caricature	hamburger	ikebana
piazza	connoisseur	virtuoso	borsch	cul-de-sac
futon	chalet	soprano	strudel	glasnost
dachshund	boutique	manga	elite	haiku
kindergarten	perestroika	frankfurter	waltz	tundra
aikido	poltergeist	cosmonaut	dojo	steppe

Japan	Russia	Germany	France	Italy

B. Fill in the blanks with the correct words from Part A.

1. My niece loves reading _____ magazines and her room is full of posters, books and knick-knacks of *Akira* and *Sailor Moon*.

2. The old house at the end of the street is said to be inhabited by a _____. People say they have heard loud noises and seen furniture moving around. But no one's lived in there for years!

3. I learnt how to bake _____ the other day. It's a pastry made with fruit rolled up in thin sheets of dough.

4. We got lost driving in the city and ended up in a _____, a dead end.

5. _____ is a form of self-defence that uses the principles of energy and motion to neutralise attackers.

6. As a rule I don't enjoy eating _____ because of its dark red colour, but I was so hungry that I gulped a whole bowl down!

7. He was a renowned _____ of fine dining, and his food reviews can make or break a new eating establishment.

8. The long-standing _____ between the two families culminated in a loud name-calling match which degenerated into fisticuffs, and the police had to be called in.

9. Today we learnt how to compose a _____, a short poem composed of three lines; the first line has five syllables, the second line has seven syllables, and the third line has five syllables.

10. Which _____ would you like in the pesto sauce — spaghetti, linguine or penne?

11. In our geography lesson today, we learnt that there are three types of _____: Arctic, Antarctic and alpine, the dominant vegetation of which is grasses, mosses and lichens.

12. I have no time to go out for lunch, so could you get a sandwich and salad for me from the _____ around the corner?

A. **The following exercise focuses on food idioms. Match the sentences with the correct idioms. These idioms can be found in the box on the next page.**

1. Soo Chin wants to involve herself in every single project.

_____

2. Providing free transport is a controversial issue in this company — the managers don't think it's necessary but the workers are all for it.

_____

3. That college only takes the very best students.

_____

4. You can't believe half the things that Sally says — she's always exaggerating.

_____

5. My little niece has boundless energy — it's so hard to keep up with her!

_____

6. My cousin's in town this month, so we'll probably spend the weekend reminiscing about old times.

_____

7. My colleague is always coming up with these new ideas but they're not very good.

_____

8. I don't feel sorry for him at all — let him suffer the consequences of his actions!

_____

9. You're going to get into trouble with the boss if you can't make the sales target this month.

10. Mr Wong works very hard to earn a living and support his family of eight.

stew in one's own juice	take with a pinch of salt	finger in every pie	cream of the crop	bring home the bacon
in hot soup	hot potato	chew the fat	full of beans	half-baked

B. I'm sure you found that a piece of cake! Now see if you can actually use the ten idioms correctly by filling in the blanks in the conversation below.

Hi, Kok Wah — guess what! I clinched the job with the design firm — no mean feat since they only accept the (1) _____. I've only been here a week but I've got to know my colleagues pretty well. There's the boss's secretary who must always have her (2) _____ — she's terrified of anything getting past her. People tell me that I must take some of the things she says (3) _____, as she tends to, you know, stretch the truth a little. Then there's good old Matt who always comes up with these (4) _____, scatterbrained ideas — nobody takes him seriously. When I came in on the first day, there was this web designer that everyone seemed to avoid — seems he's (5) _____ because of messing up some project. No one spoke to him — he's been left to (6) _____. I'm (7) _____ and raring to go — I want to show them what I can do. That means working hard and keeping clear of any trouble — like this thing about providing childcare services in the building for the workers with children — a (8) _____ if there ever was one. I know, I know, it's a huge responsibility, having to (9) _____, and with Lynda expecting our second child too.
    Well, I'll (10) _____ with you some other time, okay? Bye!

Unit 55   What A Character!

In the exercises on names we learnt how some words are derived from the names of real people. In this exercise we are going to look at fictional characters who have given rise to words that describe their character traits. For example, everyone knows that you'll never get a scrooge to lend you any money. The word 'scrooge' comes from Ebenezer Scrooge, the principal character of Charles Dickens' *A Christmas Carol*, a sour and miserly man who gets an unexpected visit from some supernatural friends.

Read the descriptions of these people and match them with their fictional counterparts.

1. Nothing ever gets her down. She's perpetually in high spirits — a hopeless optimist!

    a. Peter Pan

2. I think you should get your daughter another tutor: this one you've engaged seems rather sinister to me, and he seems to be having an excessive influence on her.

    b. Jekyll and Hyde

3. That brother of yours is a real gentleman, but to an extravagant and impractical degree — he threatened to bash up my boss for making me work overtime on my birthday, then sent me two hundred red roses to console me!

    c. Gradgrind

4. I can always count on my trusted assistant to get the necessary work done.

    d. Svengali

5. I'd stay clear of Sean if I were you — he has women after him in droves!

    e. Shylock

6. I've known Bobby for years, and he's exactly the same now as he was when he was a boy — doing exactly as he pleases, without a care in the world.

    f. Lothario

7. I can't figure him out — one moment he's really sweet and friendly and the next he's black as a thundercloud.

    g. Mrs Grundy

8. You had better not go to that loan shark — he's mean and the interest he charges will kill you.

    h. Fagin

9. My aunt is so prudish — she thinks that girls my age should be chaperoned when they go out!

    i. Man (or Girl) Friday

10. My headmaster made sure that all we did was study, study, study — he believed that acquiring knowledge was the most important thing in life.

    j. Pollyanna

11. I've never met such a brave and noble man as Damien — I didn't think there were men like him anymore in our modern times!

    k. Don Quixote

12. I read in the papers today about this man who taught school dropouts to be pickpockets.

    l. Galahad

A. Italian cuisine is more than just pastas and pizzas. The following are words commonly found on a menu in an Italian restaurant. Do you know what they are? Match the words on the left with those on the right. Make sure you don't place the wrong order and get ice cream instead of clams!

1.	antipasto	ice cream
2.	risotto	a flat bread flavoured with olive oil and topped with herbs
3.	focaccia	a sauce consisting of basil, pine nuts, garlic, olive oil and cheese
4.	vongole	coffee mixed or topped with milk or cream
5.	gelato	a rice dish cooked in stock
6.	pesto	clams
7.	carbonara	an appetiser comprising a combination of foods such as smoked meats and grilled vegetables
8.	lasagna	a strong coffee brewed by forcing steam under pressure through roasted, powdered coffee beans
9.	parmesan	a sauce containing eggs, cheese, and bacon or ham
10.	espresso	a seasoned smoke sausage
11.	cappuccino	a kind of cheese, usually grated or cut in thin slices and served as a garnish
12.	bologna	a dish made by baking fillings of meat or cheese between layers of flat pasta

B. Choose the correct option for each sentence, paying attention to the word(s) in italic.

1. If you overheard a customer ordering raspberry *gelato*, he is probably ordering
   a. an appetiser.
   b. dessert.

2. She was tucking into her spaghetti marinara with *gusto*. This means she's probably
   a. enjoying the food.
   b. forcing herself to swallow the food.

3. They are going to have an *alfresco* lunch. This means that they are going to dine
   a. outdoors.
   b. indoors.

4. You can have *linguini, spaghetti, fusilli* or *penne* with your choice of sauce. These are different kinds of
   a. pizza.
   b. pasta.

5. *Parmesan, ricotta, mascarpone* and *mozzarella* are different kinds of
   a. cheese.
   b. bread.

6. *Basil*, *oregano*, *thyme* and *dill* are different kinds of
   a. toppings.
   b. herbs.

As you know, adjectives are words that describe nouns. Some words can function as both nouns and adjectives, for example, *rubber* ball, *stone* wall, *wire* frame. *Rubber, stone* and *wire* are nouns, but they function as adjectives when they describe other nouns.

By adding a suffix (for example, *-y* or *-en*) to some of these words, we can change them to another adjective with a different, more figurative meaning. Take, for example, the word *wire*. A wire is a metallic cord which can be shaped into a coat-hanger, so producing a *wire coat-hanger*. Now what happens if you add *-y* to *wire*? You get *wiry*, a word which suggests a quality resembling wire, for example, *wiry hair* (stiff like wire) or *wiry body* (in the sense of being lean and sinewy) or *wiry tone* (resembling the sound of wire vibrating).

Fill in the blanks with adjectives formed from the words in the box below. Use each word once only.

stone	rock	silver	gold
glass	metal	ice	water
leather	cream	book	wool
wood	tin	rubber	meat
velvet	fire	wax	flower

1. I asked the waiter to take back the _____ steak – I couldn't eat it because it was so tough.

2. My tutor was annoyed with me for coming up with such a _____ argument, which lacked logic and clear reasoning.

3. She couldn't bear to miss the _____ opportunity of working in New York so she decided to go against her husband's wishes and accepted the job.

4. The couple had a big quarrel over their respective parents — what a _____ start to their relationship!

5. My legs felt _____ at the sight of all that blood, and I had to sit down for a while.

6. This bottled water has an unpleasant _____ taste. Where did you buy it?

7. Her smooth _____ voice was perfect for the jazzy melodies written for her.

8. The painter captured the _____ sunset in a blaze of crimsons and scarlets.

9. As she walked through the enchanted forest, she thought she could hear soft _____ laughter all around her.

10. The professor brought up a _____ topic for discussion that kept us engaged throughout his lecture.

11. The movie was bad in every way — lousy script, poor directing, cheap special effects and _____ acting.

12. His attempt at humour was met with blank expressions and a _____ silence.

13. He turned to me with a _____ stare, his breath reeking of alcohol.

14. He had a ghastly, pale _____ complexion, like that of a corpse.

15. He likes to use grandiloquent, ostentatious words in the _____ speeches that he prepares.

16. There have been intermittent downpours all week, with brief spells of _____ sunshine.

17. The old radio gave off an irritating _____ sound.

18. She met the principal's _____ stare with an impudent smile.

19. He's a rather shy, _____ fellow and doesn't go out much.

20. I envy her flawless, _____ complexion.

The word 'walk' in the sentence 'The little boy walks past the candy store every day' doesn't tell you much about the little boy. Now if you use 'dawdle' in place of 'walk' you have a mental picture of the boy taking his own time, looking longingly at all the sweets he wishes he could buy.

Fill in each blank with the most suitable word which represents a walking action. Choose your words from the box below and use each word once only. Some words are used as nouns instead of verbs. If it is a verb, make sure the word you use is in the correct tense.

totter	lurch	toddle	trudge	shuffle
saunter	prowl	dawdle	waddle	amble
reel	stumble	trek	swagger	hobble

1. After he was retrenched, he spent his days _____ up and down the street, looking at the shops and feeling very sorry for himself.

2. The homeless man tried on the old shoes he'd picked up from the bin, and _____ away painfully in them.

3. I know it's my neighbour walking past when I hear the _____ of his flip-flops; it's as if he has no energy to lift up his feet.

4. The drunk man _____ about unsteadily for a moment, and I braced myself to catch him in case he fell.

5. I thought that my kick to his shins would stop him, but the mean gangster _____ forward and grabbed me by my hair.

6. My two-year-old cousin came _____ down the corridor and into my arms.

7. The fat customs officer laboriously got up and _____ over to the next counter to consult with his colleague.

8. The soldiers _____ on in the rain and the mud, miserable and wet.

9. Her husband gave her a hard smack that sent her _____ to the floor.

10. The ostentatious couple _____ into the room in their opulent clothes and dazzling jewellery.

11. The _____ up the mountain was a long and arduous one.

12. There is a burglar on the _____ in this neighbourhood; several houses have already been ransacked.

13. After a good meal, we _____ back to the hotel for a shower and a nap.

14. He _____ in the dark, trying to find the light switch and cursed loudly as he stubbed his toe.

15. My niece is always scolded for _____ and being late for school.

Sounds Like ...

You have come across the term *onomatopoeia* in a previous exercise. Can you remember what it means? (Hint: the *crash* of thunder, the *roar* of traffic, the *patter* of raindrops.) That's right — onomatopoeia is the use of words that imitate the sounds associated with certain objects or actions.

A. Match the sounds with the appropriate objects.

1.	sizzle	jet engine
2.	creak	wine cork coming out of a bottle
3.	rustle	chair being dragged across a wooden floor
4.	jingle	metal dustbin cover falling on cement floor
5.	whine	pebble falling into a pond
6.	thud	wind blowing through stone columns
7.	plop	key turning in a lock
8.	pop	taffeta skirt
9.	crackle	whip being brandished
10.	scrape	feet walking on soft mud
11.	swish	car engine just before it dies
12.	clomp	coins in a pocket
13.	hum	booted feet marching
14.	whistle	sudden braking of tyres
15.	click	fish frying in a pan
16.	squeal	buttons being shaken in a tin box
17.	rattle	refrigerator running
18.	sputter	paper burning
19.	squelch	door opening on a rusty hinge
20.	clang	heavy suitcase falling from a height

B. Fill in the blanks with the appropriate onomatopoeic verbs. The first and last letter are given to help you.

1. Could you help s_____t some eye drops into my right eye?

2. The skinny boy c_____ed his way through 12 slices of apple pie and 15 egg sandwiches to clinch the prize in the eating competition.

3. I love to watch the dragonflies z_____m over the surface of the lake, their iridescent wings glinting in the sunlight.

4. The man had an irritating habit of t_____king his walking stick against the bushes as he walked along.

5. He stormed out of his bedroom and t_____ped down the stairs.

6. The boxer went down as his opponent hit him, and blood s_____ted from his cut lip.

7. I forgot that there were tomatoes at the bottom of my bag, and s_____ed the lot when I dumped my books on top of them.

8. Just leave my niece some toys — she'll play with them and b_____e away to herself in perfect contentment for hours.

9. 'I'll get you for that,' h_____sed my sworn enemy menacingly.

10. He h_____hed and shook his head in disapproval when he heard our proposal.

Shine On ... Cascade Down

This exercise focuses on words that describe light and water.

A. **Categorise the words below into words that describe the effect of light and words that describe the movement of water or other liquids.**

illuminate	swirl	ripple	shimmer
stream	glare	flash	cascade
glint	spray	lap	beam
trickle	dazzle	drip	ooze
radiate	churn	scintillate	glisten
gush	swoosh	glow	swell
gleam	rush	twinkle	sparkle
eddy	glitter	flicker	seethe

Light	**Water/Other Liquids**

B. **Fill in the blanks with the most appropriate words from Part A.**

1. The deer stood frozen in the _____ of the car's headlights.

2. During the dry season the water from the only communal tap in the poor village slowed down to a mere _____.

3. The gentle _____ of the water against the sailboat lulled me to sleep.

4. Women are said to give off a special _____ when they are expecting a baby.

5. The taxi driver behind me annoyed me by turning on his high _____ and nearly blinding me.

6. As I passed by the living room, I caught sight of the _____ing light of the television and I knew that my naughty son had crept downstairs to watch his favourite show.

7. The tourists were delighted when the humpbacked whale suddenly let out a _____ of water through its blowhole.

8. The river fell in a series of _____s down to the rocks below.

9. She stood gazing at the _____ of the lake in the moonlight.

10. His face _____ed with sweat as he finished the 10-km run.

11. She slid slowly into the water with hardly a _____ on the surface.

12. I can feel the heat _____ from the stones under our feet.

Eat, Drink And Be Merry

The words in this exercise have to do with food and eating. We hope you have a good appetite!

A. Put the words in the box below into the correct categories.

coddle	repast	ravenous	luscious
blanch	julienne	manducate	piquant
comestibles	sear	fricassee	cloying
gnaw	tangy	broil	nibble
victual	spicy	briny	viand
saute	masticate	peckish	bland
parboil	refreshments	provender	grub
succulent	simmer	peppery	tuck
famished	braise	brew	cuisine
percolate	tart	voracious	juicy
vinegary	vittles	scorch	chow

Synonyms for food and drink (nouns)

Synonyms for chew (verbs)

Words that describe the taste of food (adjectives)

Words showing methods of preparing and cooking food (verbs)

Words that describe appetite (adjectives)

B. Fill in the blank with the correct word from Part A.

1. Vivien is such a finicky eater. All she does at mealtimes is _____ at her food. Richard, on the other hand, has a _____ appetite. No matter how much he eats, he gets hungry within the hour!

2. At cooking class today I learnt how to _____ chicken; that is, cut the chicken in pieces and stew it in gravy.

3. This seafood salad has the _____ taste of the sea and may not be to everyone's liking.

4. To _____ an egg, you cook it in water just below the boiling point.

5. I just had lunch an hour ago, but I'm feeling a little _____. I think I'll order a small snack.

6. The food festival will feature the regional _____ of Italy and Spain.

7. To preserve its bright green colour, you have to quickly _____ the spinach in boiling water, then immediately remove it and put it under cold running water.

8. I'm feeling a little under the weather today, so nothing _____ for me, please. I think I'll just have some _____ porridge.

9. There will be light _____ served in the hotel lobby before the talk begins.

10. You'd better put your slippers away before the puppy _____ it.

Words Associated With Eating

blanch — to scald briefly, then drain
braise — to cook by sautéeing in fat and then simmering slowly in very little liquid
briny — having a salty taste
broil — to cook by direct heating
cloying — too sweet, therefore unpleasant
comestibles — edibles
famished — extremely hungry
gnaw — to bite and chew constantly
julienne — to cut into thin strips
luscious — juicy and delicious
manducate — to chew
masticate — to chew
parboil — to boil for a short time
peckish — slightly hungry
piquant — having a pleasantly sharp taste
provender — provisions
ravenous — extremely hungry
repast — meal, food provided at a meal

sauté — to cook in a small amount of fat or oil

sear — to grill

succulent — full of juice

tangy — having a sharp taste

viand — an item of food

victual — food supplies

vinegary — tasting like vinegar, a sour liquid

vittles — food supplies

voracious — extremely hungry

Unit 62   A Place To Call Your Own

We have seen how some words owe their existence to famous people and their achievements. All the words in this exercise are taken from place names, whether real or imagined. Such words derived from places or regions are known as *toponyms*.

A. Fill in the missing letters to form the correct toponym.

1. A pattern of motifs with swirling, tear-drop shapes. Originally from Persia and India, the pattern spread to Scotland where it was incorporated into shawls woven by the weavers of a Scottish town from which the pattern gets its name.

p		i		l		y

2. A skimpy, two-piece swimsuit worn by women. The name was coined by a French designer four days after the first atomic bomb was exploded in a test on a remote island in the Pacific Ocean. This new article of clothing took the name of the island — you could say that it exploded onto the fashion scene!

	i		i		i

3. If you say that a place is _____, it means it is full of chaotic noise, confusion and disorder. The word comes from the name of the oldest mental institution in England, Bethlem Royal Hospital.

b			l		m

4. A sparkling white wine which comes from this region in France for which it is named.

	h			p			n	

5. A _____ person is someone with a literary or artistic bent who ignores conventional standards of behaviour. From a region in the Czech Republic, the term arose in 19th century France when it was believed that gypsies, a nomadic people, came from this place.

	o		e	m			n

6. A rough fabric used to make jeans and overalls. From the city of Nimes in France, historically known for its textiles.

	e		i	

7. If someone gives you some _____ about something, it means that he or she is engaging in nonsensical, flattering talk. From the name of a stone found in a castle in Ireland which has the reputation of giving the skill of flattery to whoever kisses it!

b		a		n		y

8. When someone behaves in a _____ manner, it means that he or she is extremely self-disciplined and austere. The word is derived from a city in ancient Greece whose people lived only for war. If a baby boy was considered too weak to become a warrior, he was abandoned in the hills to die! If he was fit, he was separated from his mother at seven years to begin his military training.

s		a		t		

9. To be sent to _____ means to be shunned or ostracised. The word is derived from the name of a town in England in which a military prison was located during the 17th century.

C		v			t		

10. A common cage bird, named for the islands in the Azores from which it was introduced into Europe.

c		n		r	

B. Now see if you know the meanings of these words which are all derived from fictional place names. Match the words on the left with their meanings and origins on the right.

1. Shangri-La

    a. An impossibly perfect place in relation to its political and social organisation. From the title of the book by Thomas More, written in the 16th century.

2. Trojan horse

    b. Small-sized; tiny. From the country described in Jonathan Swift's *Gulliver's Travels*, inhabited by tiny creatures less than six inches tall.

3. Utopia

    c. A decisive conflict. Derived from the place where the battle between the forces of good and evil will take place, signalling the end of the world as prophesied in the Bible.

4. labyrinth

    d. An imaginary place of great peace and beauty, the setting for the novel *Lost Horizon* by James Hilton. When we refer to such a place, we usually take it to mean that it is a refuge from the troubles of the world.

5. Liliputian

    e. An idyllic, opulent place. Named after the place described in the poem *Kubla Khan* by Samuel Taylor Coleridge.

6. Armageddon

f. A long-distance running competition of 26 miles or 42 km. Named after the town from which, according to legend, Pheidippides, a Greek soldier, ran to Athens to announce that the Persians had been defeated.

7. marathon

g. A maze. In Greek mythology, this was the name of the maze on the island of Crete in which the Minotaur, a creature that was half-man, half-bull, was kept.

8. Xanadu

h. A subversive device placed in the enemy camp. In computer technology, a computer program in which harmful code is contained within seemingly harmless programming. Named after the city where, according to legend, the Greeks hid in a hollow wooden horse and later opened the gates to their army.

Unit 63   British Or American?

There are some differences between British English and American English. Apart from the pronunciation and spelling, certain words are more commonly used in American English compared to British English. For example, it is more common to hear an American say 'gasoline' (or simply, 'gas') instead of 'petrol'.

A. Do you know which words are in American English and which are in British English? Put them in the correct category.

yard, garden	tap, faucet	pavement, sidewalk	motorway, freeway
cookie, biscuit	truck, lorry	puncture, blow-out	rubbish, garbage
holiday, vacation	line, queue	sweets, candy	wardrobe, closet
cab, taxi	baggage, luggage	autumn, fall	elevator, lift
bill, check	curtains, drapes	baby carriage, pram	nappy, diaper
potato chips, French fries	trash can, rubbish bin	trunk, boot (of car)	bonnet, hood (of car)

British English	American English

B. Some words can cause confusion as they mean different things in British and American English. See if you can answer the following questions.

1. If an American man asks for a bill, is he more likely to be in a restaurant or a bank?

2. If a British visitor said she wanted to wash up, where would you direct her — to the kitchen or to the bathroom?

3. If an American friend asks you to hand him his vest, would you be handing him his waistcoat or his undershirt?

4. When an American tells you his office is on the second floor, how many flights of stairs must you climb?

Words We Love To Hate

So you know what synonyms are — words that have similar meanings. And you know what antonyms are — words with opposite meanings. Now can you guess what auto-antonyms are? That's right; *auto-antonyms* are words that are the opposite of themselves! An example of an auto-antonym is the word *bolt*. Bolt means both 'to hold in place' and 'to run away': *Bolt* the cage so that the rabbits won't *bolt*. Auto-antonyms are also called contranyms or Janus* words.

Fill in the blanks with the correct contranyms. The meanings of the words or phrases have been placed in brackets to help you. Choose from the box below and make sure you use the correct form.

trim	overlook	fast
cleave	table	temper
dust	scan	sanction
screen	left	handicap

1. Team A wanted to _____ (formally put up for discussion; propose) their ideas but Team B suggested that they be _____ (postponed) due to insufficient time.

2. After she _____ (removed particles of dust from) the furniture, she went into the kitchen, took out the cakes from the oven and lightly _____ (added particles of sugar to) them with castor sugar.

3. The company director _____ (approved) the internship programme for promising employees but he _____ (disallowed) the practice of giving paid leave for study.

4. His main _____ (disadvantage) is his lack of self-confidence.
   I play golf, and my _____ (the advantage that is given to someone who is not very good at the game so as to equalise the competition between this person and other better players) is 15.

5. 'I'm sure this house will hold _____ (stay firmly in one place) in the storm.'
   'I disagree — let's get out of here _____ (move quickly to another place)!'

6. 'I'm going to get Sandy to _____ (cut, in the sense of removing something from) my hair.'
   'Don't you think you should _____ (make something tidier or more level) the Christmas tree first?'

7. There was no food _____ (remaining) after the guests _____ (departed).

8. Your supervisor will _____ (superintend; oversee) your preparations for the seminar.
   You've _____ (failed to see; did not notice) one tiny detail — you got the spelling of my name wrong!

*Janus is the two-faced god in Roman mythology.

9. She _____ (examined closely) the faces in the mug book, hoping to identify the thief.
   She _____ (looked over quickly) the headlines to see if her story had been reported.

10. He used the axe to _____ (split apart) the old tree stump in two.
    The poor old lady began to _____ (cling) to her daughter-in-law when her son died.

11. He _____ (softened; made less strong) his harsh words by telling her that she was young and naive.
    The battle-hardened soldiers were _____ (strengthened) by combat.

12. He tried to _____ (hide from view) her from the cameras by holding a coat over her head.
    The new movie is going to be _____ (shown) in the middle of next month.

Think

Now That's Odd!

Have you ever wondered why we use expressions like *dust the furniture*, *shell an egg* and *peel a banana*?

Speak Up ... Pipe Down

Don't we all wish for some peace and quiet now and then? Or are you the kind of person who thrives on loud music, high-volume sounds and constant chatter? No matter — read on to acquaint yourself with some noisy and soft words. Hint: Read the words out loud, and you'll find that the sounds they make can sometimes give you a clue.

A. **The box below contains a mixture of words describing noisy, loud, unpleasant sounds and words describing quiet, soft, pleasant sounds. Put the words under the correct heading.**

hush	blaring	racket
clamorous	muffled	muted
inaudible	pandemonium	hullabaloo
deafening	pianissimo	stifled
lull	cacophony	strident
uproarious	quiescent	sough
murmur	ear-splitting	fortissimo
discordant	susurration	whisper
din	rambunctious	hubbub
dulcet	euphony	tumultous

Noisy/Loud/Unpleasant	Quiet/Soft/Pleasant

B. Some people have the gift of the gab while others have nothing much to say for themselves. Fill in each blank with the correct word. Read the clues to help you.

1. He had been very quiet at the meeting, but when the subject of charitable organisations came up, he suddenly became very _____. (7 letters beginning with 'v')

2. My father is a very _____ and undemonstrative man. When he's pleased with me, all I'll get is a thump on the back. (8 letters beginning with 'r')

3. The management is very _____ about the merger — no one seems to know anything. (11 letters beginning with 't')

4. The boys are especially _____ today; I have a splitting headache because of the noise they're making. (10 letters beginning with 'b')

5. I expect you to be forthcoming with your views on the project; instead you're being very _____. What's wrong? (15 letters beginning with 'u')

6. I asked him whether he wanted to talk about his problems, but all I got was his _____ reply: 'I'm fine'. (7 letters beginning with 'l')

7. 'Get back here,' he shouted in that _____ voice of his, loud enough to be heard in the next block. (10 words beginning with 's')

8. He protested _____ that he had a right to speak to a lawyer. (12 words beginning with 'v')

9. Don't take it personally; he's just being his naturally reserved and _____ self. (8 words beginning with 't')

10. She's a really _____ speaker, unlike the candidate before her, who had trouble putting his thoughts into words. (6 letters beginning with 'f')

When you describe something in writing, it is important that your readers could imagine them completely. You have to engage the readers' five senses and make them imagine how the thing you are writing about looks, smells, sounds, tastes and feels like. The first four senses have been dealt with in earlier exercises. Let's turn our attention now to the sense of touch.

A. **Look at the words in the box below and separate them into two categories: (1) words that describe soft and smooth objects, and (2) words that describe hard, rough and sharp objects.**

spongy	bristly	cottony	fluffy	fuzzy
sleek	prickly	wiry	stubbly	thorny
gnarled	furry	knotty	velvety	woolly
silky	jagged	downy	barbed	knobbly
serrated	brambly	spiny	satiny	fleecy
spiky	feathery			

Soft/Smooth	Hard/Rough/Sharp

B. **Read the clues to help you fill in the blank with the correct word.**

1. The _____ grass made a soft, comfortable bed for the poor homeless man. (7 letters beginning with 's' and ending with 'y')

2. I teased the fat cat by poking gently at its _____ stomach. (6 letters beginning with 'f' and ending with 'y')

3. The children love to help me to bake because they have a chance to play with the _____ cake mixture. (6 letters beginning with 'd' and ending with 'y')

4. The children had fun today in art class — they squeezed tubes of paint onto a palette, mixed the paint till it became a _____ mess, pressed their palms into the paint and made colourful handprints on white paper. (7 letters beginning with 's' and ending with 'y')

5. Be careful when you handle this old document: it's so _____ that it may crumble to pieces. (7 letters beginning with 'b' and ending with 'e')

6. Did you wash these vegetables thoroughly under the tap? They still feel _____ to me. (5 letters beginning with 's' and ending with 'y')

7. The farmer mixed the animal feed with leftover food from dinner and threw the _____ mixture to the pigs. (5 letters beginning with 'm' and ending with 'y')

8. The recipe calls for the seaweed to be boiled with water until it becomes _____ and transparent. (10 letters beginning with 'g' and ending with 's')

9. The chef grabbed the eel from the bucket but it was so _____ that it slithered out of his grasp. (8 letters beginning with 's' and ending with 'y')

10. My hair is so _____ and lustreless — I think I shall go to the hairdresser later today and get a nice perm. (4 letters beginning with 'l' and ending with 'p')

11. The man kept his leather belt _____ by polishing it regularly. (6 letters beginning with 's' and ending with 'e')

12. When a material can be stretched into a thin cord and then snap back easily to its original length, we say it is _____. (7 letters beginning with 'e' and ending with 'c')

13. Children love to play with plasticine because it is _____ and can be moulded into any shape. (7 letters beginning with 'p' and ending with 'e')

14. Put the strawberries and raspberries into a bowl and crush them with a wooden spoon until you get a _____ mixture. (5 letters beginning with 'p' and ending with 'y')

Unit 67   Which Is It?

There are pairs of words in English which are very often confused with each other. Some pairs of words are pronounced the same but are spelt differently. Others are different in pronunciation and spelling, but very similar in meaning. And still others are spelt almost the same (perhaps differing in just one letter) but have completely different meanings. Let's see how good you are at telling the difference between such confusing words.

Underline the correct word.

1. He's under the (allusion/illusion) that she's great with children when in fact she can't stand the sight of them.

2. She's an editor for a (biannual/biennial) publication — it comes out twice a year.

3. His strictness is having an (averse/adverse) effect on staff morale.

4. She was (afflicted/inflicted) by a strange disorder that made her shout out unintelligible words.

5. We have to pick a/an (uninterested/disinterested) observer to write a fair assessment of the situation.

6. Teachers should try and (elicit/illicit) answers from students rather than give them the answers directly.

7. She was irritated by the (continuous/continual) ringing of the doorbell. No sooner had she answered it, chased the salesman away and sat down than it rang again.

8. He began to entertain second thoughts about marriage as the great day became (imminent, eminent).

9. She has just bought a (luxuriant/luxurious) condominium.

10. She served a piquant salsa as a (complement/compliment) to the meat kebabs.

11. Sean is in trouble for (flaunting/flouting) the school rules.

12. The small country's (economic/economical) growth came to a standstill in the aftermath of the earthquake.

13. Can you order more (stationary/stationery) for the office?

14. He's the (principle/principal) violinist in the orchestra.

15. They are leaving today on their (historical/historic) journey into the wilds of Africa.

16. Her (ingenious/ingenuous) manner encourages people to confide in her.

17. What a thoroughly (contemptible/contemptuous) man — to run away and hide when the country sorely needs soldiers for the war!

18. Having an affair with a married man is an (amoral, immoral) thing to do.

19. My sister (immigrated/emigrated) to Australia from Malaysia.

20. 'I'm (foregoing/forgoing) dessert,' he announced virtuously.

Similar But Different!

afflicted — suffering physically or mentally

inflicted — forced someone to experience something (usually unpleasant)

amoral — having no moral principles at all

immoral — not conforming to socially accepted codes of conduct

biannual — occurring twice a year

biennial — occurring every two years

complement — to match two things together to achieve a greater effect than the two separately

compliment — to praise

contemptible — deserving lack of respect

contemptuous — showing disdain

continual — happening repeatedly

continuous — happening without interruption

disinterested — impartial

uninterested — having no interest

economic — concerned with income and wealth

economical — avoiding waste

elicit — to draw or bring out

illicit — not legally permitted

emigrate — to leave one country or region to settle in another

immigrate — to come to a country of which one is not a native, usually for permanent residence

eminent — high in rank or reputation

imminent — likely to occur at any moment

flaunt — to exhibit shamelessly

flout — to show contempt at

foregoing — previously stated

forgoing — abstaining from

historic — important in history

historical — pertaining to past events

ingenious — extremely clever

ingenuous — free from restraint

luxuriant — abundant in growth

luxurious — very expensive and comfortable

principal — main or leading

principle — an accepted rule of conduct

stationary — not moving

stationery — writing materials and office supplies

Unit 68   Words Come In Families (1)

The root of a word is the element of the word that carries its main meaning. For example, the root *cred* means 'to believe', from the Latin *credere* which means to trust or to believe. So when we add the suffix *ible* to *cred*, we get the adjective 'credible', which means worthy of belief or reliable: She gave a *credible* explanation for why she was late for the meeting, so her boss wasn't angry with her.

So if you come across an unfamiliar word which contains the root *cred*, you might be able to guess what its meaning is. Words like 'credit', 'discredit' and 'creed' belong to the same family of words.

A. Form words from the given root that will fit the definitions. The first letter of the word is given to help you.

Root: *pend*
Origin: Latin, *pendere*
Meaning: To hang, to weigh, to think, to pay out

1. a pair of elastic straps worn over the shoulders to support trousers   s _____

2. payment for the loss or damage of something   c _____

3. hanging loosely from, swinging freely   p_____

4. hanging in the air, about to occur   i _____

5. to give out, to distribute, to administer   d_____

6. to use up, to consume   e_____

7. being at right angles to the horizontal plane   p_____

8. deep in thought, reflective   p_____

Root: *quer*, *ques*
Origin: Latin, *quaerere*
Meaning: To ask, to inquire, to seek

9. the act of seeking something, a search   q_____

10. a legal investigation of the cause of a death   i _____

11. showing curiosity, asking many questions   i _____

12. to gain possession of, to obtain   a_____

13. required or necessary as a prior condition   p_____

14. a question or a doubt that needs to be answered   q_____

15. to gain or acquire by force   c_____

16. to express a desire for something, to ask politely   r_____

B. Fill in the blanks with the correct form of the words from Part A.

1. Being able to handle multiple tasks while keeping calm and collected is a _____ of this job.

2. The _____ branches swayed gently in the wind, nearly touching the surface of the water.

3. Although the native people fought valiantly, the Spanish conquistadors managed to _____ them at last.

4. He is going to get half a million dollars as _____ for having the new road cut right through his property.

5. Thus began his _____ for his long-lost brother, which ended some ten years later, when they were finally reunited.

6. The deceased's family waited anxiously for the results of the coroner's _____.

7. I'm not going to _____ any more energy fetching and carrying for you. Do your chores yourself!

8. They were all ready for the _____ arrival of the new baby — their friends and relatives had given them enough gifts to fill two nursery rooms!

9. My uncle _____ the land decades ago at a very low cost — that was how he made his fortune.

10. Could I _____ for a window seat, please?

Unit 69 Words Come In Families (2)

Here are more word families with their respective root words. This time the words are all jumbled up. Read the definition and fill in the blank on the right with the correct word. Use the contextual clues in the sentence that follows to help you.

Root: *clam*
Origin: Latin, *clamare*
Meaning: To call out

Root: *cap/cept*
Origin: Latin, *capere*
Meaning: To take, to seize

Root: *tort*
Origin: Latin, *torquere*
Meaning: To twist

Root: *volv*
Origin: Latin, *volvere*
Meaning: To roll

1. full of twists and turns

    t _____

    Their relationship is a t _____ one; one day they're throwing things at each other and the next they act as if they're the only couple in the world.

2. capable of holding a lot, roomy

    c _____

    I'm looking for a really c _____ bag — one that can hold my wallet, my mobile phone, my PDA, my lunch box and several books.

3. a loud outcry, confused noise

    c _____

    The politician's speech about the necessity of raising taxes did not go down well with the audience, and there was a loud c _____ of protest.

4. enthusiastic praise, great approval

    a _____

    His first novel was launched at the Frankfurt Book Fair to great a _____.

5. to get money using force or threats

    e _____

    It is a well-known fact that the gangsters e _____ money from the tradesmen, and those who dare resist have their shops smashed up.

6. to go round

    r _____

    The planets r _____ around the sun.

7. severe physical or mental agony

    t _____

    Some prisoners of war had to endure t _____ by their Japanese captors.

8. the development of more complex life forms from simpler ones   e _____

    Charles Darwin published his controversial theory of e _____ in the 19th century.

9. easily influenced or affected   s _____

    I'm highly s _____ to the cold weather and will break out in hives if I'm not dressed warmly enough.

10. to fascinate, to hold the attention of   c _____

    The magician was able to c _____ the children with his magic tricks.

11. to demand one's right to something   c _____

    He c _____ ed that the laptop belonged to him.

12. to rise up against authority   r _____

    The peasants were incited to r _____ against their landowners.

13. an acrobat who can twist his or her body into extraordinary positions   c _____

    Everyone marvelled at the Chinese troupe of c _____ s — one could even squeeze herself into a tiny barrel!

14. to deflect, to interrupt the progress of   i _____

    The principal i _____ ed the message that the students were passing round.

15. disgusting, repulsive   r _____

    The idea of eating meat is r _____ to Susie, who is a strict vegetarian.

16. to give a recitation, to declare dramatically   d _____

    He d_____ed the ills of materialism to a largely indifferent audience.

Words That Paint Pictures (1)

Do you know what *figures of speech* are? One of the dictionary meanings of the word 'figure' is 'outline' or 'form'. Another one is 'person' or 'individual'. These objects — outline, form, person, individual — can be seen, literally. Figures of speech, then, are words or expressions which help the readers 'see' or visualise an impression so that the readers can 'see' the incident more vividly in their mind. These words or expressions cannot be taken literally. One of the most common types of figurative language is *simile*. A simile compares two things which are seemingly unlike (for example, skin and silk), but share some feature or quality (smoothness) so that by comparing one to the other, we can vividly visualise what the writer is trying to say: *Her skin is as smooth as silk.* You need 'as', 'like' or 'than' to make a simile.

Examples:
- The puppy's eyes are as round as buttons.
- The after-rain misty forest scene, when seen from a distance, looks like a crude sketch by an amateurish artist.
- The bedsheet is whiter than snow.

There are many 'set' similes that we use every now and then: *as cold as ice, as light as a feather, working like a dog, ate like a pig.* Novelists, journalists and songwriters use similes generously so that we can conjure up the images vividly. You, too, can use similes to spruce up your writing. Be creative, though. Create your very own dish of similes to satisfy your readers' palate!

Each of the following contains a simile. Replace the underlined expression so that you now make the comparison to something else.

1. Her sadness was as <u>deep as the abyss</u>.

   _____

2. The trees bent over the grassy field like <u>weary old women</u>.

   _____

3. The mess in his room was like <u>the chaos left behind by a hurricane</u>.

   _____

4. The child was as excited as a <u>kitten running after a mouse</u>.

   _____

5. Listening to her critical remarks about my project was like <u>swallowing a bitter pill</u>.

   _____

6. Her anger grew and grew, until it burst like <u>an oversized balloon</u>.

_____

7. I feel like <u>a mat — people walk all over and take advantage of me all the time</u>.

_____

8. Her generosity is <u>as big as the ocean</u>.

_____

9. The old man gasped for air like <u>a fish out of the fishbowl</u>.

_____

10. I hate him as much as <u>a bat hates sunlight</u>.

_____

11. We simply love merry Mary and gravitate towards her like <u>moths towards light</u>.

_____

12. Completing this task is like <u>climbing a steep incline without any mountain ropes</u>.

_____

13. Her complaints are like <u>waves, constant and unending</u>.

_____

14. Jim sounded a bit offended when I told him that he was as <u>fickle as a vacillating pendulum</u>.

_____

15. Stephanie's self-control is about <u>as strong as a voracious dog with a piece of dangling meat before it</u>.

_____

16. Her heart is <u>harder than stone</u>.

_____

17. After the trying period, her mood is now like <u>sunshine bursting forth from the dispersed clouds</u>.

    _____

18. The rug felt as <u>rough as sand on a beach</u>.

    _____

19. I don't like being in this situation at all — I felt like <u>a suspect being questioned under a bright, blinding light</u>.

    _____

20. She looked forward to the days of freedom as much as <u>an emerging chrysalis about to be transformed into a butterfly</u>.

    _____

Words That Paint Pictures (2)

Like similes in the previous unit, a *metaphor* is a figure of speech which compares two unlike things, but a metaphor doesn't use 'as' or 'like' for comparison. Like similes, metaphors give vividness and variety to writing or speech. There are generally two types of metaphors.

Type 1: The metaphor takes the 'A is B' form, though, obviously, A and B are not 'visually' alike at all. In other words, the comparison is not a literal one, but suggested through the semblance of appearance or character.

Examples:
*   Her eyes are two bright buttons. (semblance of appearance)
*   Mary is my rock. She consoles me in times of trouble and is always there for me. (semblance of character)

Type 2: The metaphor lies in the verb, noun or adjective, which conjures up the figure of speech.
a.   verb: The hours *wrinkled* away.
                    She *fashioned* an elaborate lie, hoping that we'd believe her.

b.   noun: The *twilight* of her life was spent with her grandchildren.
                    Jim is in a *sea* of troubles, I'm afraid.

c.   adjective: She spoke in *icy* tones.
                    The *lazy* summer quickly passed.

Poets and songwriters use metaphors generously to appeal to readers' or listeners' senses. But don't think that metaphors are solely their business, not yours. You, too, can enliven your writing by creating your own metaphors. The key is to be creative and craft metaphors which are original and 'illuminate' the mental picture in readers' mind.

A good way to build a treasure chest of metaphors is to be more aware of the things around you and think of ways to connect them to a totally different object, thought or feeling. What does a bright sun remind you of? How about a warm bath? The surging waves? Don't be worried about whether they're Type 1 or Type 2 metaphors. If you can describe something in terms of another, you've got yourself a metaphor!

A. Each of the following contains a metaphor which makes use of semblance of appearance. Choose the most appropriate word or phrase from the list to make the metaphor.

> a Persian carpet of autumnal colours
> a landscape of hills and valleys
> an impressionistic painting of bold floral whirls and twirls
> cotton candy in the sky
> long crooked branches of an oak tree
> massive tree trunks growing close together
> mosquito coils on the forest ground
> sapphire gems
> silken threads
> the sun during the night

1. Her fingers are _____.
   They are really elongated and curved.

2. What thick legs he has! They are

   _____.

3. The field, covered with fallen leaves of muted yellows, is

   _____.

4. Her eyes are _____,
   bright and deep blue in colour.

5. The woman's face is _____,
   bearing deep scars and wrinkles.

6. The streetlamp overlooking my bedroom is

   _____.

7. The clouds are _____,
   light and soft.

8. The garden, overgrown with flaming bright flowers, is

   _____.

9. Her strands of hair are _____,
   smooth and delicate.

10. The curled-up snakes in the field resemble

    _____.

B. Each of the following contains a metaphor which makes use of semblance of character. Choose the most appropriate word or phrase from the list to make the metaphor.

fluffy wool ball	sunbeam
mist	sure-footed mule
noose around his neck	swimming pool float
sinking ship	volcano waiting to erupt
smooth train ride	warm sweater on a wintry day

1. She is furious; in fact, she is a _____.

2. My childhood is a _____. I can't remember much of what I went through.

3. My bed is a _____ when I lie on it after a day of hard work.

4. Her smile was a _____ in the dreary room full of cheerless people.

5. Her protectiveness over her son is a _____.

6. Her kindness is a woolly _____.

7. Her heart is a _____; she'll forgive you soon enough.

8. The case was a _____. I knew right from the beginning that we wouldn't win the lawsuit.

9. Unlike her turbulent past, her life is a _____ now.

10. My friend Johnny is a _____. He can manoeuvre his way through a rough terrain of difficulties.

C. Each of the following contains a metaphor suggested by the verb. Choose the most appropriate verb from the list to make the metaphor. Use the correct form of the verb.

dim	prick
drown	slice
light	snuff
massage	steal
plummet	swell

1. Her hurtful remarks _____ me; she was really insensitive.

2. Help! I'm _____ in paperwork!

3. She _____ my idea and passed it off as hers.

4. We _____ her ego before we asked her what we really went there for.

5. His ego _____ when he won the badminton championship.

6. The ratings for the reality show _____ after two of the most popular contestants were booted out of the show.

7. Her smile _____ the room of people who looked drab and cheerless.

8. The rainy weather _____ out our enthusiasm for the outing, so we stayed home.

9. The moonlight _____ the darkness and we followed the lighted path ahead of us.

10. It is a comfort that time _____ all bad memories.

D. Each of the following contains a metaphor suggested by the noun. Choose the most appropriate noun from the list to make the metaphor.

abyss	nightmare
blanket	ocean
crest	shadow
harvest	wall
loose canon	wings

1. We are drowning in her _____ of lies.

2. Her great expectations of a happy life turned into a _____ when she discovered her husband was an ex-criminal.

3. Your essay contains a rich _____ of vocabulary words.

4. The politician turned into a _____ when he was told by his own party members to step down.

5. Happiness spread its _____ when her boyfriend proposed to her.

6. The ground was covered by a _____ of snow.

7. She rode on a _____ of joy when she found out she had won the essay writing competition.

8. She fell into an _____ of misery when she found out her husband was leaving her for another woman.

9. Having made an effort to reconcile, the two of them finally tore down the _____ between them and became friends again.

10. A darkening _____ of sorrow crept across her face.

E. Each of the following contains a metaphor suggested by the adjective. Choose the most appropriate adjective from the list to make the metaphor.

breezy	scarred
decaffeinated	suffocating
fiery	tangled
flowery	whirling
salivating	withering

1. That was a _____ task. I didn't face any problems at all when carrying it out.

2. Her _____ temper will be her downfall one day.

3. The _____ mood of the guests was not helped by the depressing music that played throughout all evening.

4. Her _____ past caught up with her when her convict ex-boyfriend turned up.

5. The _____ emotions she felt after the break-up caused her much anguish.

6. The _____ memories of the tragic event remained with her for months.

7. The _____ speech, which lacked substance, did not appeal to me.

8. His zeal and _____ thirst for adventure is quite amazing.

9. _____ hopes of making our way back before sunset caused us to set up camp near the waterfall for the night.

10. The _____ crowds are making me a bit woozy.

F. Create your own metaphors. Describe each of the following in terms of another using a metaphor.

1. a woman's hair — *Her hair is a drape of silk.* _____

2. a woman's forehead _____

3. an old man's hands _____

4. someone's knees _____

5. a playful child _____

6. a difficult task _____

7. a happy day _____

8. someone's sorrow _____

9.   a friend from the past _____

10. a war-torn town _____

G. For each of the following, think of something you own, or have seen or experienced, which you can describe using the given phrase.

1.   a river — *I cried a river of tears when I heard the devastating news.* _____

2.   a rainbow _____

3.   a speeding car _____

4.   a rocking chair _____

5.   a forest _____

6.   the rising sun _____

7.   grey clouds _____

8.   jagged rocks _____

9.   a brick wall _____

10. a cat's purring _____

H. In the space below, make as many metaphors as possible using verbs, nouns or adjectives. Three examples are given for you as a guide.

• The army troops *blasted* into the building to rescue the terrorist-held hostages.
• We gazed into the night sky and surveyed the *symphony* of stars.
• We were none too pleased at the *frosty* looks the salesgirl gave us.

Unit 72 Words That Paint Pictures (3)

Human beings are unique creatures. There are many actions only human beings can do, but not inanimate (non-living) things, for example, *dance, whistle, see, kiss, nod* and *whisper*. Despite our individuality, language — life, for that matter — would be a huge yawn if human beings mind their own business and inanimate objects do their thing. Thanks to the versatility of the English language, we can give human qualities to inanimate objects — plants and abstract concepts included — so that these may be made to act like us. Why, you may ask, do we want to do this? Well, so that our imagination is richer! Look at the following examples and you'll see why.

- The plates danced on the shelf whenever a train passed by.
- The snow kissed my cheeks gently as it fell.
- The sunflowers nodded their starburst heads at one another in the gentle breeze.
- Love beckons her to accept the marriage proposal.

There — what you've seen are good examples of personification, a type of figure of speech which gives human qualities to inanimate objects or abstract concepts. Personification is often used in poetry, but you can always use it once in a while in your writing to add a vibrant and vivid touch to your prose.

A. Do the following crossword puzzle to find out what action word is used to personify the objects. Use the root word (for example, 'cough' as opposed to 'coughs' or 'coughed') to complete the puzzle. The clues to solving it are on the next page.

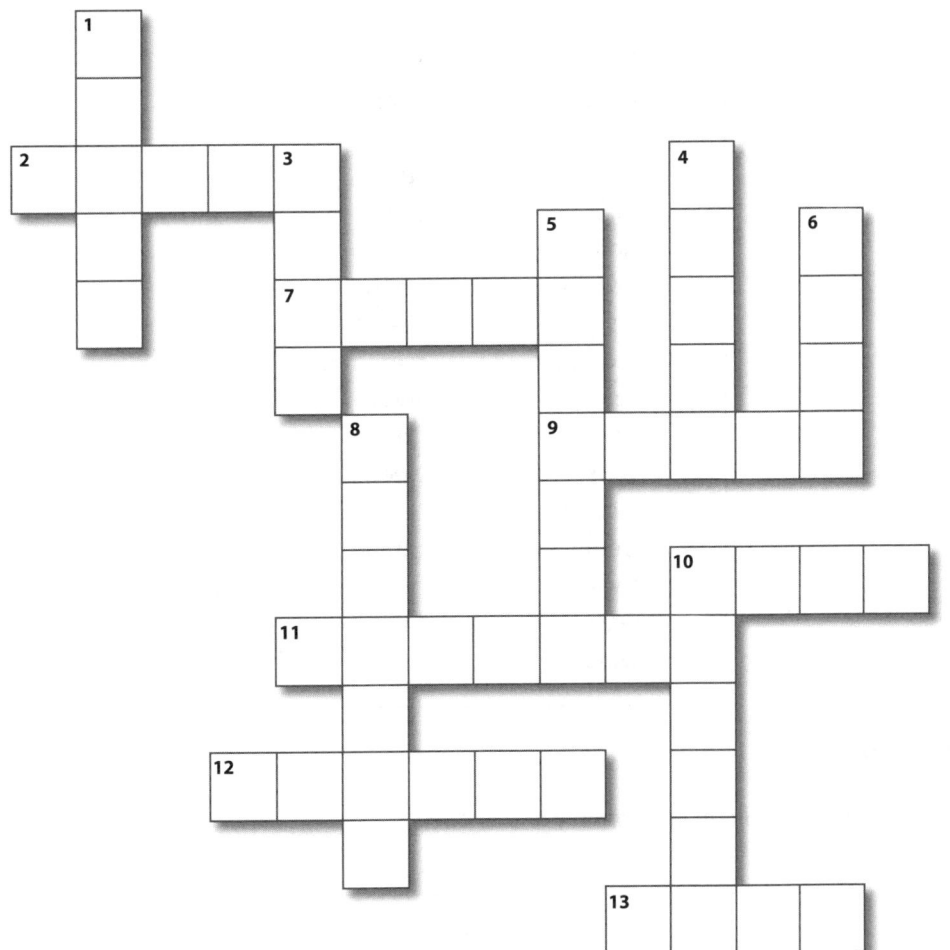

ACROSS

2 A lamppost _____ me when I turned the corner.

7 The leaves _____ in the stormy wind.

9 Her love _____ to me through her actions.

10 The winds _____ as they rushed up the hills.

11 Dad tried to start the car but it _____ by groaning in reply.

12 The sunlight _____ into the bedroom before I got out of bed.

13 The waters _____ with the pebbles at the edge of the sea.

DOWN

1 The hasty afternoon _____ towards dusk.

3 Her kindness _____ her into lending Susan the money.

4 The padlock _____ at me and challenged me to unlock it.

5 The kettle _____ a tune.

6 The raindrops on the windowpane _____ at us when we walked past.

8 The mirror _____ her, exposing bruises on her neck and back.

10 The moonlight _____ down the cobbled walkway.

B. **Now it's your turn to have a hand at personification. Choose a noun from the left-hand list and a verb from the right-hand list. Then use the pair of words to write a sentence which personifies the noun. Remember to use the correct form of the verb.**

Noun	Verb
beauty	hear
car	dream
clock	run
daffodil	skip
door	turn
drizzle	sleep
joy	see
mountain	remember
sea	sway
sky	listen
stars	weep
strawberries	tell
tree	catch
twilight	bring
waves	sing
wind	murmur

Write your sentences here.

The sea listens to the stars as they lit up the night sky one by one.

When you see the '-ist' suffix in a word, the word usually denotes a person who is an expert in a certain field, or who holds certain beliefs or who performs certain actions. If you are a *semanticist*, for example, you would have no problem doing the exercises in this book!

A. Match the following specialists with their areas of study.

1.	entomologist	eye diseases
2.	geneticist	stamps
3.	agronomist	skin disorders
4.	dermatologist	nervous system disorders
5.	toxicologist	heredity
6.	semanticist	injuries of the skeletal system
7.	numismatist	poisons and their treatment
8.	orthopedist	crop production
9.	ophthalmologist	coins
10.	neurologist	insects
11.	philatelist	blood disorders
12.	hematologist	word meanings

B. Fill in each blank with the correct '-ist' word.

1. Have you read in the news about this student at Harvard who wrote a best-selling novel but who was later discovered to be a _____? She'd copied several passages from different authors.

2. Bill is an _____ if I ever saw one — he puts the welfare of others above his own and thinks nothing of spending weekends doing volunteer work at the free clinic.

3. I think to work for the opposition party, you have to be a _____. You can't follow the crowd, and you can't be bound by what most people would consider normal practices.

4. I just had an interesting conversation with a _____ — he's a professor at the university and he's going to help me trace my family tree.

5. His brother is an _____ — he spends more than six months in a year travelling in Africa, doing missionary work.

6. My sister is a speech _____ — she helps young children who have speech defects.

7. David Attenborough is a famous _____ who has made award-winning television documentaries about animals living in their natural habitats.

8. James Thurber was a famous American _____ — he wrote about the frustrations of modern life in a humorous way.

9. A social _____ is a person who is actively involved in a variety of issues that concern society such as human rights and the environment.

10. His father was a _____ in World War I, and was imprisoned for refusing to fight.

Nothing To Fear But Fear Itself

Have you heard of people who have such a fear of a particular thing that they are paralysed when confronted with it? Such a strong, abnormal fear is called a *phobia*. For example, *arithmophobia* is the fear of numbers. You could probably have guessed the meaning by looking at 'arith', which suggests 'arithmetic' or calculations. An *arithmophobe* is someone who fears numbers.

A. Match the following with their meanings.

1.	macrophobia	fear of computers
2.	necrophobia	fear of stealing or becoming a thief
3.	cyberphobia	fear of open or public places
4.	felinophobia	fear of colours
5.	agoraphobia	fear of cats
6.	chromophobia	fear of confined spaces
7.	claustrophobia	fear of long waits
8.	kleptophobia	fear of death or dead things

B. Choose the correct word from the pair of words given. (You will see that there is also a phobia word for fear of fear itself!)

1. acrophobia — fear of (food, heights)

2. cynophobia — fear of (swans, dogs)

3. arachnaphobia — fear of (rats, spiders)

4. autophobia — fear of (automobiles, loneliness)

5. entomophobia — fear of (worms, insects)

6. hematophobia — fear of (blood, sweat)

7. hydrophobio — fear of (gas, water)

8. hypnophobia — fear of (sleep, waking up)

9. microphobia — fear of (germs, dust)

10. mysophobia — fear of (travelling, dirt)

11. ophiciophobia — fear of (crocodiles, snakes)

12. pathophobia — fear of (hospitals, disease)

13. pedophobia — fear of (adults, children)

14. phasmophobia — fear of (ghosts, fear)

15. phobophobia — fear of (happiness, fear)

16. photophobia — fear of (dark, light)

17. teratophobia — fear of (monsters, dinosaurs)

18. wiccaphobia — fear of (brooms, witches)

19. xenophobia — fear of (strangers, friends)

20. zoophobia — fear of (zoos, animals)

We have just seen that the suffix *-phobia* is used to construct words that describe an irrational fear. Its antonym is the suffix *-philia*, which is used to describe the love for or obsession with something. For example, *logophilia* is the love for words; *logophiles* are extremely interested in word games like *Scrabble* or doing crosswords. They even enjoy reading mundane things like labels!

C. Match the following with their meanings.

1. biophilia   love of England and all things English

2. bibliophilia   love of movies

3. anglophilia   love of nature

4. cinephilia   love of books

Now that you know what *-phile* and *-phobe* stand for, what do you think *philophobia* means?

Unit 75 And The New Word Is ...

English is a living, changing language. New words and expressions are being created all the time, and whether these new words become acceptable or not (and eventually make their way into the dictionary) depends on their frequency of use.

A. Match the words or phrases on the left with their meanings on the right.

1.	biometrics	a.	involving active participation in contrast to knowing something in theory only
2.	digital divide	b.	violent behaviour shown by drivers, usually when they are under stress
3.	makeover	c.	a terrorist who kills himself or herself (usually with a bomb), along with the victims
4.	carjacking	d.	the gap between those who have Internet access and those who do not, or the gap between those who are computer literate and those who are not
5.	road rage	e.	a middle-aged person who enjoys engaging in youthful pursuits
6.	sound bite	f.	easy to use
7.	hands-on	g.	the identification of an individual using biological traits like fingerprints, iris and retinal patterns and facial features
8.	blog	h.	the taking of a vehicle by force or intimidation
9.	suicide bomber	i.	a financial backer who provides venture capital for entrepreneurs
10.	angel investor	j.	an overall beauty treatment to improve the appearance or image of a person
11.	cross-trainer	k.	letters sent through the postal system, as opposed to e-mail
12.	snail mail	l.	a website that contains dated entries by a contributor (from the words 'We**b**' and '**log**')
13.	user-friendly	m.	a shoe designed for various sports
14.	adultescent	n.	a short, quotable statement suitable for a television or radio news programme

B. Now see if you understand how the words or phrases are used by filling them into the correct blanks.

1. _____ is a hot topic of research now — as apparently it is a more secure form of authenticating a person's identity than typing in passwords.

2. These days the tax forms are designed to be _____ — I normally finish filling up mine in minutes.

3. Statistics show that incidences of _____ are on the rise — what is it about driving that turns some people into monsters?

4. He was fortunate to get the _____ to provide him the capital for his start-up company.

5. The workshop will provide your employees with the _____ experience they need. They will get to actually use the equipment to do their assignments.

6. I cannot imagine using _____ anymore, not when sending e-mail is so fast and convenient.

7. I could hardly recognise Shelby in those _____ photos she had taken — she looked like a film star!

8. To capture the attention of the audience, the politician was advised by his spin doctor to make his comments in _____.

9. It is no wonder that _____ are very popular: by keeping one, you can convey information, feelings and opinions to people all over the world.

10. This whole range of expensive new computer games is designed to capture the _____ market — who can afford to pay for them in contrast to their younger counterparts.

Some among us hold very definite views about the issues around us. Look at the following list of names ending in '-ist' which we give to people. Then match each to the statement which he or she most likely utters.

masochist	nonconformist	exhibitionist
narcissist	hedonist	lobbyist
idealist	pragmatist	reformist
fatalist	bigamist	chauvinist
optimist	alarmist	fundamentalist
pessimist	recidivist	misogynist
nationalist	socialist	misogamist
activist	altruist	misanthropist
atheist	racist	escapist
anarchist	pacifist	romanticist
perfectionist	imperialist	sadist

1. I want changes. I'm all for changes. Change is the only constant!

2. I don't believe in God.

3. They all say I am overemotional and maudlin. You could say I am a sentimentalist, too.

4. I know it's not possible to eradicate poverty altogether, but I believe that we should show unselfish concern for the welfare of others.

5. Eat, drink and be merry. Live like there is no tomorrow!

6. I hate women. Why do you think I don't have woman friends, not to mention a wife?

7. Call me a dreamer if you like but I am positive that we can turn this world into a paradise where there are no human suffering and diseases.

8. I hate marriage.

9. I admit I like to subject myself to pain, or unpleasant or trying experiences.

10. On the other hand, I like to inflict pain on others.

11. I live alone. I don't talk to my neighbours. I dislike people in general. I don't trust them at all.

12. We are the better sex. I'd only have a male take over my job.

13. I'm the only one who doesn't — or won't — wear a tie to a formal party. On the other hand, I might turn up in a suit when everybody is in jeans and T-shirts.

14. I look on the bright side of life all the time.

15. I'm the complete opposite: I think about the worst in life. I'm not surprised if the world ends tomorrow.

16. It doesn't matter what I do. I can't change my destiny.

17. No true-life human dramas or war stories for me, please, but give me a fantastic tale to read anytime to get away from real life.

18. I am — ahem — full of admiration for the person I see in the mirror.

19. Migrate to another country? Not in a million years! My country is the most superior in the world.

20. Don't just sit there rattling on about social injustice; do something about it — like us!

21. I refuse to fight in a war. I don't believe in taking another human life.

22. I've just been convicted of the criminal offence of marrying a woman while legally married to another.

23. I expect 100 per cent score for your maths test, Peter — 100 per cent, no less.

24. A group of us is trying to persuade the government to stop the proliferation of nuclear arms.

25. I may do headstands on the street just to get people's attention.

26. I take a sensible and practical approach when solving problems.

27. My race is more superior than yours.

28. I often put fear and anxiety into people needlessly by spreading false rumours of impending danger.

29. I've been punished enough, but I just don't learn my lesson and continue with my criminal acts.

30. I believe that everything should be owned by the government and that everyone should have an equal share of the country's wealth.

31. What can the government do for us? The legal system is useless. Abolish all government laws — that's my view!

32. I strongly stand by the view that there's nothing wrong with expanding our influence by defeating and acquiring other territories.

33. I adhere to my religious laws and principles very strictly.

Part 2

Tackling the Vocabulary Question in the GCE 'O' Level English Language Paper 2

Language is a city to the building of which every human being brought a stone.

Ralph Waldo Emerson

Inferring Word Meanings From Context

It would be very cumbersome if we have to look up the dictionary every time we come across an unfamiliar word in an article. What some of us do is to 'gloss over' the word since our understanding of the word does not affect our comprehension of the article. Most of us, though, use the context to help us decipher the meaning of the word. The context of a word is the group of words or sentences surrounding that word. If you don't understand what that word means, you can often infer its meaning by looking at the context. The 'clues', or hints, that the context provides can help you to determine the meaning of the word.

So, don't be intimidated by the vocabulary question in the GCE 'O' level English language paper. Examiners, or for that matter writers, are not monsters in devil's suits who want to make your life miserable by giving you difficult 'clueless' words to find meanings. If you're discerning enough, you can often find the contextual clues that help you to determine the meaning of a word.

The key is to be a detective who is called to the scene of a crime. In the same way he examines the surroundings and looks for clues to uncover all the pieces of evidence to figure out what happened at the crime scene — they dust for fingerprints, look under rugs, collect blood specimens at the scene, wander through grimy tunnels if they have to. You don't have to go to such lengths, of course, to find the meaning of an unknown word; what you need are basic detection skills to find the meaning of a word.

The following are common types of contextual clues which can help you discover the meaning of an unfamiliar word.
* Definition and restatement
* Example
* Antonym
* Synonym
* Logic

Sometimes more than one type of contextual clue will be given to help you uncover the meaning of a word. Units 77 to 81 explain how each of these clues may be used to unlock the meanings of unknown words with exercises for practising these skills. Units 82 to 98 are a consolidation of these skills.

Note that, like the words tested in the vocabulary question in the English language paper, each of the words tested in the units may be explained in a word or a phrase of not more than seven words. You are therefore encouraged to do the same when replacing each word.

Sometimes a writer may define a word to give readers a clearer understanding of it. At other times, the writer may restate an idea in different words in the same sentence or in another sentence. This type of clue is the easiest to spot. Words such as *or* and *that is* often signal a word definition or restatement of ideas. The definition/restatement of ideas may at times follow a comma, colon or dash, or it may be set off by a pair of commas. Watch out for all these punctuation clues.

Study the following example. What words give you a clue as to what the italicised word means?
- *Sedentary* workers, people who are deskbound or inactive, should exercise more than those in active fields.

Even if you don't look up the dictionary, you know that 'sedentary' means 'deskbound or inactive' because the writer has defined it for us. We call this type of contextual clue a 'definition' clue.

Sometimes, a writer restates an idea in other words so that an unfamiliar word becomes recognisable.

Take a look at the following example. What does the italicised word mean?
- I couldn't blame the students for showing *apathy* — a lack of interest — in class today because it was the last day of the term.

Again, if you don't know the meaning of the word 'apathy', the phrase 'a lack of interest' restates the idea of apathy and provides a contextual clue to its meaning. This type of contextual clue is called a restatement clue.

Study each of the following sentences. The italicised word is defined somewhere in the surrounding text. In some instances, the idea contained in the italicised word is restated in another phrase. You don't have to be a first-rate detective to figure out the meanings of these words!

1. Aunt Maggie likes *kohlrabi*, a vegetable related to the cabbage.

   kohlrabi _____

2. The government promised to *augment*, or increase, job opportunities.

   augment _____

3. Zebras live in *savannahs*. These grassy plains are also home to many other wild animals.

   savannahs _____

4. Beauty is an *evanescent*, or temporary, thing.

   evanescent _____

5.	She leads a very *hectic* life. That is, she is always very busy and rushing about.

	hectic _____

6.	She gave us a *vapid* expression: dull and lifeless.

	vapid _____

7.	The actor Gregory Peck was the *quintessential* mid-century American man — he was the ideal American man: tough and good-looking.

	quintessential _____

8.	Meg is rather *saturnine*, or melancholy, in nature.

	saturnine _____

9.	What is your stand regarding *euthanasia*, the killing of a person for merciful reasons?

	euthanasia _____

10.	The agency was involved in some *covert* activity. No outsiders knew anything about its secret operations.

	covert _____

Context may help us tremendously in understanding the meaning of a word by listing one or more examples. In this type of clue, watch for key words like *such as* and *for example* which signal examples.

Here is an example. What do you think the italicised word 'lustrous' means?
- Several *lustrous* objects brightened up the room, for example, the glittering crystal chandelier, the sparkling silver china on the table and the glimmering chrome sculpture at the corner of the room.

In the above example, a list of things given as examples helps you to understand the meaning of 'lustrous' — 'glittering' or 'glimmering'.

Look at the sentences below. Are you familiar with the words in italics? Don't you worry if you're unsure about their meanings. Look at the given examples, give it a little thought, and — yes! — we're sure you'll unlock the meanings of the words.

1. The war museum contains some excellent examples of war *memorabilia*, such as flags, cannonball, maps, guns, photographs and uniforms, all related to the country's military past.

    memorabilia _____

2. A photographer's *paraphernalia* includes strobe lights, umbrella diffusers, light stands and tripods, and huge seamless rolls of paper.

    paraphernalia _____

3. This class was full of *precocious* children. One child could read before she started nursery school and another could do algebra at seven.

    precocious _____

4. He's such a *bigot*! One of his beliefs is that only males are allowed to rule the world.

    bigot _____

5. The government will only use the relief funds for *exigencies* such as in times of floods or earthquakes.

    exigency _____

6. Steve's *scrupulous* attention to detail, such as using British spelling throughout and differentiating between the 'short' hyphen and the 'long' dash, will make him a good editor.

    scrupulous _____

7. The police uncovered many *macabre* objects at the scene of murder: hoods and masks, a metal skull, and a phial of what was believed to be human blood.

    macabre _____

8. Places of *egress*, such as the plane's doors and detachable windows, must be clearly labelled.

    egress _____

9. His writings were so *lucid* you can easily follow his arguments at the first reading.

    lucid _____

10. Kim is the *anomaly* in our family. For example, last week, we all agreed on New York as the vacation destination, but Kim insisted that London was a better choice; the other day, all of us headed for the beach after a week of dreary weather, but she opted to stay home.

    anomaly_____

Unit 79 Antonym

By contrasting an unfamiliar word with something familiar, a writer can help you to find the meaning of the unfamiliar word. You might, for example, find the antonym or an opposing idea for the word. The key is to look out for signal words such as *but*, *unlike*, *in contrast to*, *on the contrary* and *however*.

Here is an example. What do you think the italicised word 'reticent' means?
- Karen is usually talkative and lively, but she was quite *reticent* at the party.

The connector 'but' signals a contrasting of ideas between 'reticent' and 'talkative and lively'. From this, we can guess that 'reticent' is the opposite of 'talkative', that is, it means 'reserved' or 'quiet'. The hint provided here by the context is called an antonym clue.

Using antonym as contextual clue, find the meanings of the words in italics.

1. Unlike John's crystal-clear explanations, Peter's reasons were rather *nebulous*.

   nebulous _____

2. I *concur* with you on the implementation of the new policies but I disagree that we should put them in place so soon without feedback from the staff.

   concur _____

3. *Avarice* is different from other kinds of greed in that its main object is money.

   avarice _____

4. While George is easily understood by others, his brother is *inscrutable*.

   inscrutable _____

5. The clean and clear water of the nearby lake is a stark contrast to the *turbid* air in the distance.

   turbid _____

6. The children are always sluggish and cheerless on schooldays, but when Sundays come, they turn *ebullient* at once.

   ebullient _____

7. Kelly has complete faith in her ability, while Mary is more *diffident* in nature.

    diffident _____

8. I didn't give the holiday plans much thought and decided quickly on my choice of country to visit. On the other hand, Julie *ruminated* on them before stating her preference.

    ruminate _____

9. I reacted to her accusation without *rancour* whereas Peter was spiteful and hostile towards the allegation.

    rancour _____

10. We expected our new colleague to be serious and humourless, but he turned out to be quite a *jocular* fellow.

    jocular _____

Unit 80 Synonym

Here again, by comparing the unfamiliar word with something more familiar, a writer can give you a key to help unlock the meaning of the unfamiliar word. You might, for example, find the synonym or synonymous phrase for the word. The key is to look out for signal words such as *like*, *similarly*, *also* and *in the same way*.

Here is an example. What do you think the italicised word 'exuberant' means?
- Like Tiffany, who is always high-spirited and cheerful, Cheryl is *exuberant* all the time.

The word 'like' signals a similarity in ideas contained in the words 'exuberant' and 'high-spirited and cheerful'. From this, we can guess that 'exuberant' means 'high-spirited and cheerful'. The hint provided here by the context is called a synonym clue.

Using synonym as contextual clue, find the meanings of the words in italics.

1. Like his previous novel, which received terrible reviews, his latest book was an *execrable* piece of work.

    execrable _____

2. Like any other beginner, a *novice* in the kitchen will make mistakes.

    novice _____

3. The woman was sure her kidnappers had a *nefarious* plan to kill her by throwing her into the river — or some equally evil means — if the ransom was not met.

    nefarious _____

4. William Shakespeare and Agatha Christie were two *prolific* authors, having produced many works which fill several shelves in most libraries.

    prolific _____

5. In his first book, the author gave an *authoritative* account of the revolution; he approached the second book in a similar fashion, and the end product is a highly reliable account of the aftermath of the uprising.

    authoritative _____

6. Bedouin are traditionally an *itinerant* tribe; similarly the West African Tuareg were once nomads, travelling from place to place.

    itinerant _____

7. My mum is a *gregarious* woman; my dad, too, is outgoing and sociable.

   gregarious _____

8. Her *morose* mood was in the vein of that day: glum and miserable.

   morose _____

9. The mountain air was *pristine*, not polluted.

   pristine _____

10. Last week, Irene *connived* with Damian to play a trick on Matthew. This week, they did it again: they conspired to set a trap for John.

    connive _____

Unit 81 Logic

Our experience with life and common sense can tell us many things. We may not understand a particular word in a sentence or paragraph, but we can make an intelligent guess about its meaning by drawing conclusions based on common sense or logic. Though we do not understand the unfamiliar word, we know what the writer is trying to say generally because he/she gives us a 'familiar' context to help us make a fairly accurate guess about the meaning of the unknown word.

Look at this example.
*   Much to my *chagrin*, the job interview wasn't successful and I didn't get the job.

From real-life experiences, we know that not getting a job is a disappointing affair. So logic tells us that in the above sentence 'chagrin' means 'disappointment'.

For each of the following, study the context for logic clues before you figure out the meaning of the italicised word.

1. Halfway into the late night movie, Sam's mother noticed the *somnolent* expression on his face and ordered him to bed immediately.

   somnolent _____

2. My sister, Gina, is my *nemesis*: she beats me in everything — from sports to academic subjects.

   nemesis _____

3. 'I don't care where we go for the holidays,' I told him. 'The *crux* of the matter is can we afford it?'

   crux _____

4. When I told Myra that I felt lethargic nowadays, she said, 'Go for a swim now and then. It's a *salutary* exercise for everyone'.

   salutary _____

5. 'Those grey clouds *portend* rain,' Jill said. 'I think we'd better head back.'

   portend _____

6. Joshua was *inundated* with homework when his teachers each assigned a demanding project to be completed over the weekend.

   inundated _____

7. After the plague, the floods *exacerbated* the farmer's misery of a difficult year.

   exacerbate _____

8. 'Mum, I'm not being difficult!' Donna *remonstrated*. 'I did tell you I wasn't going to Uncle Ted's house and nothing is going to make me go now.'

   remonstrate _____

9. A true coffee *aficionado*, she'll scour the town for the best coffee places whenever she's overseas.

   aficionado _____

10. The *inimical* relationship between the two states has heightened tension among the surrounding countries.

    inimical _____

Unit 82 Four-Letter Words

In a previous unit, we learnt some three-letter words. In this unit, we focus on four-letter words. Don't undermine short words — they carry as much weight as long words and can deliver a deadly punch to a sentence, which long and so-called 'impressive' words may not.

The following list of four-letter words is worth a second look. Study the context and figure out the meanings of the words.

1. I like Susan for her cool demeanour. She has the *mien* of keeping things under control.

   mien _____

2. Although he was not directly involved in the robbery, he was charged with *abetting* the robbers by helping them to escape in his car.

   abet _____

3. Investigations revealed that he had been *bilking* the company of nearly a million dollars over a period of three years.

   bilk _____

4. Little Red Riding Hood *wended* her way through the forest to Grandma's house, little realising that she was followed by the cunning wolf.

   wend _____

5. Asked why he had punched the youth in the eye, he *averred* that he had acted in self-defence: the young man had attempted to strike him but he dodged and threw a punch on his face to protect himself.

   aver _____

6. When my brother learnt that I had driven my car up a kerb during my driving test, he *jibed* at me until I issued a threat: stop taunting or I'd take back all the music CDs I lent him.

   jibe _____

7. Despite his friends' attempts to *goad* him into taking his first cigarette puff, Timmy knew better and refused to do so.

   goad _____

8. It was difficult to implement ideas and see them through as the company was in a state of constant *flux*.

    flux _____

9. The government deal was *mired* in controversy as allegations of corruption surfaced and officials were sucked into the bog of another scandal.

    mire _____

10. Even though she said she didn't care a *whit* about the science test, we knew that she did, or she wouldn't stay up all night cramming for it.

    whit _____

Don't be left behind in the world of politics and economics — build a strong working vocabulary in these disciplines in order to keep up with the changes in the world.

Start with the following list! You might find these words in the newspapers every now and then. Study the context and figure out the meanings of the words.

1. For the first time since the country gained independence, employment rate surpassed 75 per cent. Never in its 30-year-old history had the country enjoyed such *unprecedented* economic growth.

    unprecedented _____

2. Either apologise formally by midnight today or be sued — that was the party's *ultimatum* to the opposition.

    ultimatum _____

3. The election campaign turned out to be an *acrimonious* affair, marked by rancorous and bitter exchanges among the political candidates.

    acrimonious _____

4. Differences in ideologies between the old and the young threatened to divide the party into two factions; opposition parties were expected to use this *schism* as a trump card to win over voters.

    schism _____

5. After the prime minister was *apprised* of the latest situation in the Middle East, he decided to cancel his trip there.

    apprise _____

6. This community practised an *esoteric* form of Christianity; little is known or understood of it by people outside the commune.

    esoteric _____

7. Three days of bombing completely *obliterated* the town, leaving behind a trail of bloody remains and debris.

    obliterate _____

8. Employment has hit its lowest and skilled workers are even willing to take the most *menial* and lowest paid jobs.

    menial _____

9. The people demanded more directness from the public transport company on the question of an expected fare hike, while all the public transport spokesman had been doing was to give *oblique* answers to their questions.

    oblique _____

10. The defendant, *putative* mastermind of the series of bombings on the resort town, entered the courtroom with a vacant expression on his face. Alleged to be the perpetrator of the terrorist attacks, he could be sentenced to death if found guilty.

    putative _____

Legal Eagle

In case you're wondering, a legal eagle refers to a lawyer. Many legal terms (for example, *prima facie*) have Latin origins. Even if you don't intend to become a lawyer, it's good to know some legal terms so that you can talk about human rights — and your own, of course.

The list of words used here forms a lawyer's lingo. Study the context and figure out the meanings of the words.

1. I bought this insurance policy which *indemnifies* my house against accidental hazards such as fire and burglary.

    indemnify _____

2. I believe she's going ahead with the legal proceedings; she'd rather *litigate* than settle out of court.

    litigate _____

3. His political opponent *impugned* his account of what happened at the rally but he made no attempt to defend his version of what his rivals claimed was a sham.

    impugn _____

4. I can't be at the meeting to vote in the new committee, so I suppose I'll get Joshua to be my *proxy*.

    proxy _____

5. After his lawyer's advice that there was a high chance of losing the case, the *plaintiff* decided to drop the suit.

    plaintiff _____

6. The unwilling witness was served with a writ and *subpoenaed* to appear in court.

    subpoena _____

7. The lawyer has yet to inspect the case more deeply, but as of now, there is a *prima facie* legitimate claim against their employer.

    prima facie _____

8. His lawyer informed him that since the pieces of antique he had stolen were worth thousands of dollars and that since they could not be recovered as he had sold them, he might be charged with grand *larceny*.

   larceny_____

9. At the end of the trial, the court found out that the governor lied under oath and charged him with *perjury*.

   perjury _____

10. The colonel, wanted for war crimes against his people, was *extradited* to his native country so he could stand trial before his own people.

    extradite_____

Life isn't always a tough cookie. As the following words show, life has its genial and glorious moments too. Study the context and figure out the meanings of the words in italics.

1. When the usual *rubicund* colour returned to her face, I knew that she had returned to her good health.

    rubicund _____

2. The team looked set to lose yet another game as the score stood 3-0 against it; the *propitious* moment came when its striker scored a goal in the opening minute of the second half.

    propitious _____

3. She felt a sudden aura of *numinous* peace as she sat in the pew and listened to the hymns being sung.

    numinous _____

4. A holiday amidst a *sanative* setting of sea and fresh air will restore me to my healthy spirits, I'm sure.

    sanative _____

5. Her fiery personality seemed to be the only thing *coruscating* in the sad and gloomy conditions surrounding her.

    coruscate _____

6. We could not completely erase human suffering, but we could at least *ameliorate* living conditions to make the earth more habitable.

    ameliorate _____

7. The excessive inflow of funds for the tsunami victims testified to the *plethoric* kindness of the community.

    plethoric _____

8. She was raised among *indomitable* women: strong, resolute and unconquerable.

    indomitable _____

9. I worry too much and lose sleep over the most trivial matter. I wish I were more like my sister, with her *blithe* spirit.

    blithe _____

10. Mother Teresa, who devoted most of her life to helping the poor and sick, was a *paragon* of virtue.

    paragon _____

Unit 86 Stop The Pain

You might come across the following words in an article discussing pains and anti-pain strategies. A good way to learn vocabulary is to note all the specific words associated with a particular theme. Then, when you have to write about the topic, you can list down all these words and consider how you may use them to expand on the topic.

For the following words in italics, study the context before you figure out the meanings.

1. Almost all of us have experienced pain from our internal organs. Indeed, a *visceral* pain, for example, a stomach upset or chest pains, is the number one reason to consult a doctor.

    visceral _____

2. *Unremitting* diseases, such as cancer and arthritis, destroy body tissue and are associated with chronic pain.

    unremitting _____

3. The *analgesic* drug morphine is often used in patients with terminal cancer for its powerful pain-relieving effects.

    analgesic _____

4. Before the *advent* of modern painkillers, women in labour chewed on objects such as sticks or rags to deal with the pain. The arrival of anti-pain drugs such as nitrous oxide provided great relief for these women.

    advent _____

5. One of the difficulties doctors face in helping their patients to manage pain is its *subjectivity*. That is, pain is a personal experience, and doctors may underestimate the patient's pain.

    subjective _____

6. A patient may complain of a pain and the doctor may think that it is all in his mind and that he is *malingering*, even though he is really in some form of pain and not acting up in order to avoid work.

    malinger _____

7. Ask a person suffering from a chronic pain to find a *redeeming* feature in his pain, and he will probably say, 'How can there be 'goodness' in pain? How can anything compensate for pain?'

    redeeming _____

8. Some form of pain is good. Pain sends a message to *alert* us that something is wrong.

    alert _____

9. The aim of pain management programmes is not so much to eliminate pain completely from the patients, but to help patients cope with it by assisting them to live a normal life without *exacerbating* the pain.

    exacerbate _____

10. The world will not be completely free from pain, but doctors and 'carers' of the world are trying to reduce the suffering of the countless men and women who have to go through *abominable* physical pain every day.

    abominable _____

Toughing It Out

Let's face it — life isn't a bed of roses. Life is often tough, harsh and difficult. The words here reveal the difficult side of life, so you have to tough it out a bit. Study the context and figure out the meanings of the words.

1. I felt *inexorable* doom when the beast pounced on me, gripped me relentlessly and sank its fangs into the crevice of my shoulder.

   inexorable _____

2. It was *adamantine* resolve that made her leave her abusive husband and start life afresh: she had since never once yielded to the thought of a reconciliation with him.

   adamantine _____

3. How did we fare in the competition? I can only say that our *puissant* opponents reduced us to a group of weak, fumbling fools.

   puissant _____

4. It's such a *Sisyphean* task teaching that class of students who are not motivated to study at all.

   Sisyphean _____

5. The room was filled with a *sepulchral* silence when we heard that the president had died.

   sepulchral _____

6. I was assigned the wearisome chore of greeting the guests; I preferred the less *onerous* task of just bringing out the food.

   onerous _____

7. He had to put up with the *squalid* overcrowded apartment until he could afford a clean and decent apartment in a nice district.

   squalid _____

8. The old man remained *obdurate*, refusing to lend his son a single cent despite the latter's pleas for help to clear his debt.

   obdurate _____

9. All the colleagues, envious of the promising newcomer, conspired to *beleaguer* him until he was forced to leave the company.

    beleaguer _____

10. The child takes a *diabolical* pleasure in abusing cats.

    diabolical _____

Though there are comparatively few words which start with the letter 'Z', they are worthy to be among the vocabulary gems in your memory bank. Here are some words we have sieved out just for you. Study the context and figure out the meanings of these words.

1. The *zaftig* French actress confessed that on account of her size, she wasn't really suited to play the heroine, a role based on a fiction character who had a willowy and slender frame.

    zaftig _____

2. The children laughed hysterically when the three *zany* comedians appeared and performed their crazy acts.

    zany _____

3. They have the kind of weapons that can *zap* the enemy from thousands of miles.

    zap _____

4. Kim had become a *zealot*, committing herself to the human rights organisation and fervently championing for freedom of speech.

    zealot _____

5. *Wall Street*, a movie about material wealth taking precedence over morality, reflects the *zeitgeist* of the 1980s in the US: the power of money drives the economy.

    zeitgeist _____

6. There were many high points in his career, which reached its *zenith* in 1989 when he became the town mayor.

    zenith _____

7. The fantastic dragon-slaying tale I'm reading turns out to be quite a good read. I've just reached the part where the dwarf shuffled gently into the forest, like a *zephyr* rustling through leafy trees, to confront the draconic beast.

    zephyr _____

8. I've been so broke lately that when Dad asked me how much I had with me, I said, 'Zilch'.

    zilch _____

9. The bland food was more than compensated by the conversations which flowed with *zing* and laughter.

    zing _____

10. I was *zonked* after the 12-hour non-stop flight to Toronto.

    zonked _____

The words in this unit are all associated with noise, be it loud or soft, harsh or genial. They may be nouns, verbs or adjectives. How many do you know? Study the context and figure out their meanings.

1. We sat through two hours of his *diatribe* against modern Western imperialism and wished that we were at another table instead and did not have to put up with the verbal attacks.

   diatribe _____

2. She did not shed a single tear, not until the moment they lowered the coffin into the freshly dug grave, and then a tiny sob, which gave way to an *ebullition* of tears.

   ebullition _____

3. What a pompous speech! That *rodomontade* of his about his political stance is more a chance to blow his own trumpet than a call to arms.

   rodomontade _____

4. Grandma's *dulcet* tones often soothed Peter to sleep no matter how tired he was.

   dulcet _____

5. Dad oiled the door hinges to *obtund* the squeaky noises.

   obtund _____

6. The street was buzzing with the *cacophony* of honking cars, screeching tyres, yelling mothers telling their children to come home, children hollering back, hawkers shouting out their wares.

   cacophony _____

7. I found out from our holidays together that she was such a complainer: she *kvetched* about the weather, the food, the service, the traffic — there was nothing she wouldn't whine about!

   kvetch _____

8. 'I'm afraid I have to hang up now,' Mrs Todd told the caller. 'My *vociferous* son is demanding a bedtime story before he can go to bed.'

   vociferous _____

9. Knowing that his mum will be enraged when she discovered he had broken her favourite vase, Tom tried to think of a way to *mollify* her.

    mollify _____

10. Even from our bedroom upstairs, we could hear Uncle Ted's *stentorian* voice coming from the kitchen.

    stentorian _____

We often use French words without our knowing it. For example, when you're in a restaurant, the waiter might ask whether you'd have the buffet, that is, eat all you can from the delicious spread and pay only a fixed price for it, or an a la carte meal, that is, order from the menu and pay a separate price for each dish. The words 'menu' and 'a la carte' are from French.

The italicised words in this unit are all French words. Study the context to find the meaning of each.

1. We admire Mrs Todd for her *savoir-faire*; she's the perfect hostess at parties, for example, saying all the right things and making everyone feel at home.

    savoir-faire _____

2. 'That costume is a bit *outré*,' my sister said of my attire. 'Don't you think it's bizarre, Mum?'

    outré _____

3. 'When things are great at home, they aren't so at the office. When office life is sunny-side up, things are anything but great at home,' she sighed. 'Oh well, *c'est la vie*!'

    c'est la vie _____

4. I felt a distinct sense of *déjà vu* as I walked into the room. The weighty chandeliers and the thick maroon curtains looked strangely familiar.

    déjà vu _____

5. I prefer works by *avant-garde* artists, not ordinary and unimaginative pieces by the mainstream majority.

    avant-garde _____

6. We were amazed at her *insouciance* as she strolled into the hospital to collect her medical examination results.

    insouciance _____

7. I was *piqued* by Jane's criticism that I looked monstrous in that green attire and stomped off to my bedroom to change into a more agreeable outfit.

    pique _____

8. After two weeks at home nursing a broken ankle, she felt a sense of *ennui* settling in and was eager to return to the hustle and bustle of office life.

    ennui _____

9. I doubt those fellows in the top *echelon* know what we the working class on the lower levels do.

    echelon _____

10. The teacher told us to write a *précis* of the article. 'Keep it short and include only the main ideas,' she stressed.

    précis _____

11. James refuses to help out with the project! The next time we have a meeting I will have to reprimand him about his *laissez-faire* attitude.

    laissez-faire _____

Italian Words And Phrases

In a previous unit, we came across some words connected with food and cooking that are of Italian origin. Besides a healthy measure of words, English has borrowed many artistic and musical terms from Italy, home to music and arts. In this unit, we shall learn some common Italian words and phrases.

Study the context and figure the meanings of the words.

1. The actor didn't want to be recognised by the paparazzi, so he wore a wig, put on a fake moustache and travelled *incognito*.

   incognito _____

2. The members of the press were specifically warned not to ask about the actress's divorce, but one overenthusiastic reporter did and got into an *imbroglio* with the actress, who wasn't too pleased that the complicated heated argument got reported in the papers.

   imbroglio _____

3. It was a gradual effort — our art collection was acquired *a poco a poco*.

   a poco a poco _____

4. The fashion show was attended by the local *cognoscenti*, all eager to see the designs of the art students and to share their knowledge with them.

   cognoscenti _____

5. Julie told me *sotto voce*, in case anyone was within earshot, that she would be coming home late and that I was not to tell Mum and Dad about it.

   sotto voce _____

6. Though it caught me by surprise, the *salvo* of praises I got from my usually reticent family members for winning the spelling competition pleased me tremendously.

   salvo _____

7. Persian rugs, Rembrandt paintings, Ming vases — these possessions reveal the owner to be a man of *vertu*.

   vertu _____

8. She is only a young actress but is already acting like a *prima donna*, demanding that everyone be at her beck and call.

    prima donna _____

9. What a *virtuoso* performance! The cellist was deserving of all the adulation and applause for his personal style and masterful musical skills.

    virtuoso _____

10. The choir was so used to singing with the piano accompaniment that they needed a little getting used to when they sang *a cappella*.

    a cappella _____

Unit 92   Latin Words And Phrases

In this unit, we shall study some Latin words and phrases in context. Although now widely considered a language which is no longer in use, Latin has had a major influence on many modern languages. Many Latin words are found in medical and legal jargon. Once a while, they crop up in normal speech and writing. You might have heard or seen some of these words in action before, but did not quite understand what they mean. Well, after this exercise, you will!

Study the context surrounding the following Latin words before you reason out the meanings.

1. What a bore — he's going on and on *ad nauseam* about his political views. I wish someone would shut him up!

    ad nauseam _____

2. Unless there is significant political or economic reform, I'd rather the government preserve the *status quo* in the country.

    status quo _____

3. Everyone thought it was a *bona fide* Rembrandt he bought but it turned out to be a fake.

    bona fide _____

4. Ever since he was prohibited from entering the country for political reasons, he has been *persona non grata*.

    persona non grata _____

5. Simon, a friend I haven't seen for a long time, turns out to be my *alter ego* — we have the same disposition and share the same interests and tastes.

    alter ego _____

6. Sometimes, when we're in the middle of a discussion, Dad would add a funny *non sequitur* which has totally no relevance to what we said.

    non sequitur _____

7. My sister and I have a *quid pro quo* arrangement about clothes: she lends me hers and I lend her mine.

    quid pro quo _____

8. The monkey *in extremis* gave a shrill cry before it collapsed on its side and died.

   in extremis _____

9. You can't get them to talk to each other; she hates him, and *vice versa*.

   vice versa _____

10. The Russian writer Leo Tolstoy's *magnum opus* is *War and Peace*, deemed by many critics to be the greatest novel ever written. His other masterpiece is, of course, *Anna Karenina*.

    magnum opus _____

11. Everyone thought the hero was doomed, until a *deus ex machina* popped up in the form of a stranger who helped him to safety.

    deus ex machina _____

12. Rather than relying on *ad hoc* decisions, we should form a consistent plan for dealing with emergency situations.

    ad hoc _____

Ten Adjectives To Know

Look at the following two sentences:
*   The man parked his car in the parking lot.
*   The *lanky beardy* man parked his *rusty* and *dilapidated* car in the *empty secluded* parking lot.

Which sentence conjures a more vivid image? The second one, surely. By using adjectives (words in italics), the man, car and parking lot are given more form and definition. Without adjectives, the image is one-dimensional, but with specific words to describe the nouns, it now has a three-dimensional effect and we can see the picture more vividly. So, weave adjectives to good effect into your writing.

Below are ten good adjectives to know. Study the context and figure out the meanings of the words.

1. Rather than meeting regularly, our meetings consisted of the odd, *desultory* dinners which stopped altogether after Christmas.

    desultory _____

2. There was a *specious* brightness about her voice. I perceived that this unnatural sing-song ring in her low tenor voice was an attempt to disguise her disappointment at not being offered the job.

    specious _____

3. I had expected a promising evening with good food and merry company, but the *ominous* shift in the weather in the late afternoon put our plans in jeopardy.

    ominous _____

4. He was his characteristically quiet self until three beers later, when his *aberrant* behaviour gradually emerged to the amusement of everyone.

    aberrant _____

5. Whenever Mr Finn changed from a relaxed to a *peremptory* or urgent tone, we hushed up and did our work quietly and quickly.

    peremptory _____

6. He ran up *stupendous* debts through huge losses in the stock market.

    stupendous _____

7. She had seen so many museums that she found herself indifferent to the surroundings of this one and looking at the exhibits in a *nonchalant* manner.

   nonchalant _____

8. Unlike the perky and cheery person she used to be before the divorce, she now constantly wore a *dolorous* expression on her face.

   dolorous _____

9. I've always been a *prodigious* eater. It's my sister who eats like a bird.

   prodigious _____

10. When Mary accused me of letting her secret out, I put up a *vehement* denial: 'I did not! You know you can trust me to keep a secret!'

    vehement _____

Adverbs are words that modify (describe) verbs (action words). For example, 'quickly' is an adverb: She walks *quickly*. You can see that adverbs have a sense of control over verbs — they tell verbs how to behave. If adverbs aren't bossing the verbs around, you may find them modifying and associating themselves with adjectives (*extremely* beautiful) or other adverbs (*very* quickly). Note that most adverbs are formed by adding '-ly' to adjectives.

Below are ten good adverbs to know. Study the context and figure out the meanings of the words.

1. The soldiers opened fire *sporadically* at the insurgents. We heard gunfire echoing from the hills at odd times of the day.

    sporadically _____

2. Your story is *superfluously* long; there are too many details which are not essential to the main plot.

    superfluously _____

3. She spoke *poignantly* about the past, but I am one who is unsentimental or unemotional about the old days.

    poignantly _____

4. You won't believe how *parsimoniously* he lived now considering what an extravagant person he used to be.

    parsimoniously _____

5. She greeted the guests *perfunctorily*, wishing that her mother had not assigned this role of welcoming people she did not know and had not the least interest in.

    perfunctorily _____

6. The minister's ignorance of the viral scourge was lambasted by the health community when he commented *spuriously* that there was no immediate danger of an epidemic.

    spuriously _____

7. She could feel someone watching her *surreptitiously* as she waited in the hotel lobby and this unnerved her.

    surreptitiously _____

8. 'I should have believed her when she said she didn't steal the money,' Grace said *ruefully*. 'After all, she's my best friend.'

    ruefully _____

9. The detective questioned her *relentlessly* until she lost her composure and confessed to the crime.

    relentlessly _____

10. Roland reads *voraciously*. I've never once seen him without a book in his hand.

    voraciously _____

What are we to do without nouns? While adjectives and adverbs are like the herbs and spices that add pizzazz to the flavour, nouns are the 'meat' of the sentence: it is what gives sustenance to our communication. We speak about people, places and things every day, and we use words to name them. There are also things we speak about which we cannot see — ideas and feelings. A word that gives a name to a thing is called a noun. Below are ten good nouns to know.

Study the context and figure out the meanings of the words.

1. Aunt Maggie is a *polyglot*: she can speak English, German, French and Italian.

    polyglot _____

2. Though her family expressed concerns, she was prepared to deal with the social *stigma* of raising her child as a single mother.

    stigma _____

3. She said with all *candour* that she wished she were at home watching *American Idol* rather than meeting us.

    candour _____

4. I will have no *compunction* firing her from the job; she is easily the laziest and most incompetent employee who has ever worked under me.

    compunction _____

5. While the other speakers gave lacklustre and dispassionate speeches, Jenny's presentation was delivered with *ebullience* and flair.

    ebullience _____

6. After a long *hiatus* from work, John decided to look for a job.

    hiatus _____

7. A *paucity* of supplies forced the hikers to head back to their camp down the mountain a day earlier than scheduled.

    paucity _____

8. Joseph is not inclined towards tidiness and I'm afraid his *proclivity* to disorder will not go down well with Aunt Susan with whom he is staying for a while.

    proclivity _____

9. The politician took *umbrage* at the suggestion that he had used government funds to further his personal interests.

    umbrage _____

10. He got all of us into serious trouble, but he showed not the least *contrition* for his actions.

    contrition _____

Ten Verbs To Know

A verb expresses an action (seen or unseen) or a state of being.

Action (seen):   She *stomps* out of the house.
Action (unseen): Tom *expects* a promotion soon.
State of being: The mango *tastes* juicy.

An idea cannot be completed without a verb. You might say that verbs keep the nouns very busy. Good writers know how to use verbs to enliven their writing. So use vivid and specific verbs to give a lucid and graphic mental picture for your reader. Below are ten good verbs to know.

Study the context and figure out the meanings of the words.

1. The minister's reputation was *tarnished* by his involvement in the bribery scandal.

   tarnish _____

2. The prisoner, who was sentenced to death by hanging, shed tears of relief when he was *reprieved* at the last minute.

   reprieve _____

3. We were fuming mad when we spent 15 minutes trying to get the attention of a waiter to serve us. When we were finally noticed, the apologetic head waiter *placated* us by telling us that he would serve us coffee and some ham sandwiches on the house at once.

   placate _____

4. The judgement of this case demonstrated the fairness of the judge and *manifested* his constant sense of impartiality and even-handedness.

   manifest _____

5. We were amazed at the devious way the incompetent and ineffective Peter *manoeuvred* his way to the top to become the chairman of the company in such a short time.

   manoeuvre _____

6. Isabelle just can't decide whether to go to London or Rome for the holidays. She's still *vacillating* between the two options.

   vacillate _____

7. He was convicted of manslaughter but new evidence uncovered by the police *vindicated* him of any wrongdoing.

    vindicate _____

8. Sadly, the recalcitrant behaviour of the party members *stultified* the credibility of its party, which they had built up over the years.

    stultify _____

9. The whole evening she *enthused* about her invitation to the actors' award ceremony.

    enthuse _____

10. The man *aggrandised* his financial situation by marrying the wealthy woman, much to the disapproval of the latter's family.

    aggrandise _____

The following list of words comprises the level and type of vocabulary you can expect to be asked in the vocabulary question in the GCE 'O' level English language examination paper (refer to Part 3 for a more exhaustive list). Most of these words should look very familiar to you, though to explain them in context may be a little tricky.

In this unit, we have put each word in two different contexts — the differences in meaning may be subtle and you need to use precise words to convey the contextual meaning. Now, study the context and figure out the two meanings for each word.

1. a. After the attack, he was *assailed* by nightmares and had not been sleeping well since then.

    assail _____

    b. Critics *assailed* his third novel, calling it 'literary trash'.

    assail _____

2. a. The necklace *chafed* against my neck, causing a small outbreak of rashes there.

    chafe _____

    b. James was *chafed* at me when I turned up one hour late.

    chafe _____

3. a. Scientists *detected* high levels of mercury in that lake.

    detect _____

    b. I *detected* a note of sarcasm in her remark though I might attribute that to my having a more sensitive nature than most people.

    detect _____

4. a. Is there a *remote* possibility that you decide to stay even though you are all packed to leave the country?

    remote _____

    b. It took hours to find that *remote* town. It's certainly well hidden away!

    remote _____

5. a. His cautiousness *verges* on timidity. I wish he would loosen up a little and take some risks.

    verge _____

    b. The prison grounds *verge* on the nearby forest park.

    verge _____

6. a. The hunters *traced* the wounded tiger to the clearing and lay in wait for it behind the bushes.

    trace _____

    b. The detectives found *traces* of blood in the corridor leading to the bedroom where the murdered body was found.

    trace _____

7. a. The appliqué, embroidery, beads and lace — I really love the *embellishments* on this quilted bag!

    embellishment _____

    b. When the account of the incident finally reached me, I wasn't sure whether it was a true report or just a fanciful story heightened by *embellishments* through the retellings.

    embellishment _____

8. a. She has such an *infernal* temper that we stay clear of her whenever possible.

    infernal _____

    b. This fantastic tale surrounds a fallen magician newly empowered with *infernal* powers of darkness to bring doom to mankind.

    infernal _____

9. a. We didn't enjoy ourselves at the hotel at all. There was discomfort all round as the conditions there were *primitive* and there was lack of modern amenities.

    primitive _____

    b. Archaeologists have unearthed some artefacts here, suggesting the existence of a *primitive* village on the spot thousands of years ago.

    primitive _____

10. a. The five days of strike by the postal workers *culminated* in the government's surrender to their union's demands for higher pay and better working conditions.

culminate _____

b. Tension reached its peak when the pockets of armed resistance *culminated* in a full-scale war.

culminate _____

Here are more words you should know before you tackle the GCE 'O' level English language examination. Again, meanings of pairs of words are designed in context for you to figure out their definitions.

1. a. She is a very pragmatic person. She *contemplates* a problem from all angles before she settles on the best possible solution.

    contemplate _____

    b. He *contemplated* resigning from his work and going overseas to further his studies.

    contemplate _____

2. a. I expected him to give me an incredible excuse for coming late yet again, but his explanation that he fell into a pit did seem *plausible* when I saw the bruises on his arms and legs.

    plausible _____

    b. He's a smooth talker — a *plausible* rogue — so he may be lying!

    plausible _____

3. a. My grandfather's health has been *declining* over the years. Now he is even too weak to walk and needs a walking stick.

    decline _____

    b. I *declined* the job offer but wondered, on second thoughts, whether I should have accepted it.

    decline _____

4. a. The new mobile phone model *penetrated* the local market to be the number one bestselling phone after only two years.

    penetrate _____

    b. Thanks to technology, science has *penetrated* the mysteries of space and the universe and given us a greater understanding of the world we live in.

    penetrate _____

5. a. Once a populous and vibrant town, it is now a *desolate* land, deserted and bleak, without a soul in sight.

    desolate _____

    b. While her sister is cheerful and lively, Maureen looks *desolate* all the time.

    desolate _____

6. a. Her death was *shrouded* in mystery; no one really knew what happened, and not even the detectives were able to fingerprint the exact cause of death.

    shroud _____

    b. It was customary in this village to cover a corpse with a *shroud*, a cloth made of sack material, before it was buried.

    shroud _____

7. a. You should have been there to hear the cheers and roars that went off at our school stadium when our school football team scored the winning goal against our biggest *rival*, St Thomas Secondary School.

    rival _____

    b. No one can *rival* Jonathan's oratorical skills. Even the best speaker in the school debating team cannot match his oral facility with the language.

    rival _____

8. a. The plants *flourished* under the tender care of Mrs Greenfinger.

    flourish _____

    b. Goldie ran into the room, *flourishing* a letter. 'I'm accepted by Yale University!' she shouted, the piece of paper fluttering in her hand.

    flourish _____

9. a. There is a *significant* change in the tax laws and companies are expected to make major adjustments in their accounting policies as a result.

    significant _____

    b. There has been a *significant* increase in bus fares, which will affect commuters considerably.

    significant _____

10. a. She follows the trend and won't be caught dead wearing an outfit which is out of *fashion*.

    fashion _____

    b. We were amazed when Dad, who has great carpentry skills, *fashioned* a table out of a pine log.

    fashion _____

Analysing Word Parts To Determine Meaning

In the preceding section, you looked at contextual clues, that is, the surrounding words or sentences, to determine the meaning of an unknown word.

In this section, you shall see that sometimes you need not look further than the word itself to infer meaning — the word itself may contain information that can tell us its meaning. This information lies in the word parts.

A word may be broken down into three main parts:
* Root
* Prefix
* Suffix

Knowing the meaning of these individual parts can often help us to understand the meaning of the whole word.

The **root** (or stem) is the base word to which prefixes and suffixes are added. Many root words are derived from Greek or Latin. (Note that you were introduced to root words in Units 68 and 69.)

A **prefix** is placed at the start of a root and often changes its meaning.

A **suffix** is added to the end of a root and changes the way it is used (for example, a suffix can change a verb into a noun).

Example:

Prefix	Root	Suffix
in	aud	ible

In the example above, the root *aud* means 'hearing', the prefix *in* denotes 'not' and the suffix *ible* makes the word an adjective. So *inaudible* means 'not being able to be heard'.

Units 99 to 101 encompass skills to unlock the meanings of words through word parts. Use these skills, together with contextual clues, to find the meanings of unknown words you may come across.

Root Words

Look at the meaning of the root words in the box below. Then read the sentences, and, using your knowledge of the root words and making use of contextual clues, guess the meanings of the words in bold.

loqu; locut	speak
amat	love
mal	bad
stell	star
psych	mind
corp	body
fid	faith, trust
ten	hold
tang	touch
vor	eat

1. The old matriarch kept a *tenacious* grip on the affairs of her children; nothing ever escaped her notice.

    tenacious _____

2. The play tonight has only one actor who is going to, hopefully, entertain his audience with an hour-long *soliloquy*.

    soliloquy _____

3. To breed cattle, you need a large acreage, as cattle are *graminivorous*.

    graminivorous _____

4. In the film, Wilson is in love with the female protagonist but she rejects his *amorous* advances.

    amorous _____

5. The politician was greatly *maligned* by the press for his involvement in the bribery scandal.

    malign _____

6. She wanted all the *tangibles* — a car, a house and a rich husband — and determined to get all three within five years.

    tangibles _____

7. He's been having severe headaches but after a thorough checkup, the doctors still cannot find out what is wrong with him. They are beginning to suspect that his symptoms are *psychosomatic*.

    psychosomatic _____

8. *Infidelity* is a common cause of marriages breaking up.

    infidelity _____

9. I arranged the fruit sticks in a *stellate* pattern, and everyone commented on what a spectacular display it was.

    stellate _____

10. Many people believe that our *corporeal* existence is unimportant; what matters is the state of our souls.

    corporeal _____

Look at the meaning of the prefixes in the box below. Then read the sentences, and, using your knowledge of the prefixes and making use of contextual clues, guess the meanings of the words in bold.

ante-	before
counter-	against
extra-	beyond
neo-	new
hyper-	above or too much
quasi-	seeming or like
retro-	backwards
tele-	at a distance
ambi-	both, double
geo-	relating to the earth

1. My feelings about the new student leader are *ambivalent*; he's articulate and personable but there's something about his manner that I don't quite trust.

    ambivalent _____

2. My present job allows me to *telecommute*, which is ideal for me as I live in the suburbs.

    telecommute _____

3. The use of gunpowder in fireworks by the Chinese *antedates* that of the Europeans' use of it as weapons.

    antedate _____

4. I think making employees work extra-long hours is *counterproductive* — people need to relax after a hard day's work.

    counterproductive _____

5. This week's episode of *The X-Files* was about a girl who possessed *extrasensory* perception.

    extrasensory _____

6. In *retrospect*, I should have apologised at once and not let our friendship break up.

    retrospect _____

7. *Geothermal* power is now generated in over 20 countries, with Iceland using it to produce 17 per cent of its electricity.

    geothermal _____

8. She is fond of using *hyperbole* in her writing — too much, in fact!

    hyperbole _____

9. In computer lingo, a *neophyte* is known as a 'newbie'.

    neophyte _____

10. When he couldn't get a job as a researcher, he decided to publish his own *quasi-scientific* magazine.

    quasi-scientific _____

Look at the examples below of noun, verb, adjective and adverb suffixes. Then read the sentences. Identify what part of speech the word in bold is before writing its meaning.

Some Noun Suffixes

Suffix	Example
-age	lineage
-ary	seminary
-ment	government
-ion	adoption
-ism	hedonism
-ist	abolitionist
-ity	laxity
-ness	lateness
-ship	dictatorship

Some Verb Suffixes

Suffix	Example
-ate	stagnate
-ify	signify
-ise	economise
-ite	unite

Some Adjective Suffixes

Suffix	Example
-able/-ible	commendable/eligible
-al	dictatorial
-ful	thankful
-ic	scenic
-ine	feline
-ive	preventive
-ish	childish
-ous	prosperous
-less	thoughtless
-ile	tactile
-ant	deviant
-ate	irate

Some Adverb Suffixes

Suffix	Example
-ly	tentatively
-wise	clockwise

1. A monkey has a *prehensile* tail, which acts like a fifth hand and can be used to manipulate objects.

    prehensile _____

2. He had the *temerity* to question the principal's decision to report the matter to the police after he was caught red-handed with the missing cash in his locker.

    temerity _____

3. I was told only at the last minute that I needed to give a speech, so I suddenly had to *improvise*.

    improvise _____

4. My heart sank at the sight of the *saturnine* official checking the forms. I suppose it being a gloomy Monday didn't help his mood.

    saturnine _____

5. I couldn't stand my colleague's *puerile* behaviour — one would expect a 30-year-old woman to be more mature than that.

    puerile _____

6. My boss made a *cryptic* remark as he left the office that made us all wonder.

    cryptic _____

7. Not only do I suffer from short-sightedness, but I also have a very high degree of *astigmatism*. And now it appears that my long-sightedness is increasing as well!

    astigmatism _____

8. He *vehemently* denied that he had anything to do with the prank.

    vehemently _____

9. Being named 'Businesswoman of the Year' was the *culmination* of all her hard work and sacrifice.

    culmination _____

10. My brother is fond of giving long lectures that are meant to *edify*, but they just bore me to tears.

    edify _____

11. She found herself in a *quandary* when she had two job offers and did not know which one to accept.

    quandary _____

12. The opposition leader is well respected for being a *sagacious* and honest man, who resisted the baiting of the ruling party.

    sagacious _____

13. The saying 'Power tends to corrupt, and absolute power corrupts absolutely' suggests that we should be aware of man's *propensity* for abusing his power.

    propensity _____

14. The police knew that the private detective was a *perspicacious* fellow — that was why they engaged his help to solve the most baffling of crimes.

    perspicacious _____

15. The *obdurate* gambler spent his last few dollars on the horse races, even though he had been persistently losing in all his gambling activities for the last few months.

    obdurate _____

16. The teacher's prompt action *obviated* the need to report the matter to the police.

    obviate _____

17. The new polytechnic is different from older, more traditional ones as it employs *heuristic* methods of learning.

    heuristic _____

18. There was a *palpable* sense of horror in the observers' room when the prisoner was strapped to the electric chair.

    palpable _____

19. The *zeitgeist* of 1980s America was a belief in the power of money.

    zeitgeist _____

20. He was passed over for the promotion because of his *lackadaisical* attitude.

    lackadaisical _____

When One Word Will Not Do …

For the vocabulary question in the GCE 'O' level English language paper, you are required to give one word or short phrase of not more than seven words to replace the given word. It is sometimes difficult to find an 'exact' synonym to replace the word. When that happens, you may have to explain it using a short phrase.

Using '-ing' phrase to explain meaning

As an example, you are asked to give one word or short phrase which has the same meaning as 'charismatic' in the following sentence.

- Franklin D. Roosevelt and Martin Luther King were two *charismatic* leaders the world had witnessed.

The thesaurus lists a few words synonymous with 'charismatic': 'magnetic', 'compelling', 'captivating', etc.

These words, unfortunately, do not embody the spirit of 'charismatic' in this context. A charismatic leader possesses an extraordinary quality associated with leadership. So, in essence, 'charismatic' means 'possessing an extraordinary quality associated with leadership'. Note that we can use the '-ing' form of the word 'possess' to begin the short phrase which explains the meaning of 'charismatic'.

More examples:
- His **culinary** skills won him the 'Chef of the Year' competition.
  (Analysis: Culinary skills *concern* cookery. → culinary: *concerning* cookery)

- The manager's **laudatory** remarks about her performance encouraged her to work even harder.
  (Analysis: Laudatory remarks *give* praise. → laudatory: *giving* praise)

Using 'the state of …' or 'the quality of …' phrase to explain meaning

Sometimes it is useful to explain the meaning of a noun (a word which names a state, quality or condition) using the phrase 'the state of', 'the quality of', 'the condition of' or a similar expression. Study the following examples. What do the words in bold mean?

- The author lived in **oblivion** after writing his last novel and was never seen or heard of ever since.
  (Analysis: oblivion → the state of being utterly forgotten)

- The lack of **symmetry** in the building's exterior is at odds with its interior's structural balance.
  (Analysis: symmetry → the quality of showing a balanced form)

After completing Units 102 and 103, you will have a general idea on how to explain the meaning of a word in terms of the phrases you learnt above.

Unit 102   Using '-ing' Phrase To Explain Meaning

Look at the list of adjectives in the left-hand column below. Each of them may be explained by a short phrase in the right-hand column. Note that all the phrases are in the '-ing' form. Match the adjective with the phrase. Hopefully this exercise will give you an idea on how you can use an '-ing' phrase to replace a word, when you can't find a one-word synonym for it.

1.	efficacious	a.	remaining free from dirt or decay
2.	ulterior	b.	expressing sorrow or sadness
3.	corporeal	c.	producing the desired outcome
4.	pristine	d.	relating to agriculture
5.	censorious	e.	causing an emotional reaction in the listener
6.	cerebral	f.	appearing genuine but actually not
7.	cloistered	g.	living a sheltered life
8.	venerable	h.	showing hesitation
9.	tentative	i.	possessing many dimensions
10.	plaintive	j.	having material existence
11.	euphonious	k.	lying beyond a recognised boundary
12.	vacuous	l.	wishing evil on another person
13.	prudent	m.	posing a serious threat
14.	evocative	n.	lacking content or substance
15.	pernicious	o.	exercising due care
16.	malevolent	p.	appealing to the human mind
17.	multifaceted	q.	tending to cause great harm
18.	malignant	r.	pleasing to the ear
19.	agrarian	s.	commanding reverence
20.	specious	t.	finding fault easily

Look at the list of nouns in the left-hand column below. Each of them may be explained by a short phrase in the right-hand column. Note that all the phrases begin with 'the state of', 'the quality of' or a similar expression. Match the noun with the phrase. Hopefully this exercise will give you an idea on how you can begin the explanation of a word meaning using such phrases when you can't find a one-word synonym for it.

1.	transience	a.	the quality of being splendid
2.	nonchalance	b.	the condition of being outdated
3.	severance	c.	the quality of having been untrue
4.	transgression	d.	the act of disbanding
5.	infidelity	e.	the quality of being old
6.	disparity	f.	the quality of being puzzled
7.	celibacy	g.	the state of being cut
8.	bemused	h.	the act of going beyond set limits
9.	cessation	i.	the quality of being pure
10.	grandeur	j.	the quality of being brief
11.	relevance	k.	the condition of suffering
12.	obsolescence	l.	the act of becoming sorry for shortcomings
13.	kibosh	m.	the quality of being motionless
14.	ebullience	n.	the act of stopping
15.	dissolution	o.	the quality of being pertinent
16.	concurrence	p.	the quality of being unconcerned
17.	adversity	q.	the act of drawing to a close
18.	antiquity	r.	the quality of being enthusiastic
19.	stagnation	s.	the condition of being in agreement
20.	contrition	t.	the condition of being unequal

Part 3

GCE 'O' Level Words
You Should Know

Colours fade, temples crumble, empires fall, but wise words endure.
Edward Thorndike

The list of words below are essential words to know before you tackle the GCE 'O' level English language paper. Match each word with its meaning by writing down the word or phrase in the blank.

A

abandon	_____	abnormality
abashed	_____	accomplish
abhor	_____	add to
abscond	_____	amazing
abundance	_____	appeal to
accede	_____	appropriate
accelerate	_____	ashamed
accumulate	_____	attack
acute	_____	build up
adamant	_____	change
adroit	_____	conceited
advance	_____	consent
affluent	_____	dry
alleviate	_____	evident
alter	_____	hate
ameliorate	_____	ill will
angle	_____	improve
annual	_____	increase in value
anomaly	_____	large quantity
antipathy	_____	leave behind
aplomb	_____	lessen
apparent	_____	make off
appreciate	_____	move forwards
apt	_____	point of view
arid	_____	resolute
arrogant	_____	self-confidence
assail	_____	serious
astounding	_____	skilful
attain	_____	step up
attract	_____	wealthy
augment	_____	wrong
awry	_____	yearly

B

baffle	_____	advantage
banished	_____	aggressive
banter	_____	band
barely	_____	boldness
baulk	_____	bring up
bear	_____	captivate
beguile	_____	completely without hope
belligerent	_____	confuse
belt	_____	curt
bereft	_____	exiled
besotted	_____	only just
boon	_____	refuse to do something
brandish	_____	restrain
bravado	_____	smitten
breach	_____	tease

bridle   _____   tolerate
broach   _____   violation
brusque   _____   wave

C

carnivorous   _____   acclaim
censure   _____   agree
chafe   _____   all the time
chief   _____   as a result
clearly   _____   at this time
compliant   _____   attentiveness
concentration   _____   aware
concur   _____   conforming
conscious   _____   criticise
consequently   _____   cut back
constantly   _____   end
contemplate   _____   express
convey   _____   meat-eating
cover   _____   most important
credit   _____   necessary
crucial   _____   protection
culminate   _____   scrape
currently   _____   think about
curtail   _____   without a doubt

D

debility   _____   aloof
decline   _____   contrasting
deduce   _____   course
defunct   _____   departure
demonstrate   _____   deteriorate
dense   _____   different
depict   _____   gloomy
deserted   _____   infer
desolate   _____   order
detached   _____   out of use
detect   _____   overshadow
deviation   _____   represent
devise   _____   rundown
dictate   _____   show
dilapidated   _____   shrink
diminish   _____   solitary
direction   _____   spot
disparate   _____   steadfast
diverse   _____   thick
dogged   _____   weakness
dominate   _____   work out

E

efface   _____   alluring
effectively   _____   appear
egregious   _____   blown up
emancipate   _____   compensate
embellishment   _____   confirmation

emerge	_____	conspicuously bad
eminent	_____	decoration
enticing	_____	disentangle
entire	_____	enlarge
epitome	_____	fair
equitable	_____	flight
escape	_____	set free
eventually	_____	sooner or later
evidence	_____	successfully
exaggerated	_____	typical example
expected	_____	useful
expedient	_____	usual
expiate	_____	well-known
extend	_____	whole
extricate	_____	wipe out

F

fade	_____	clean
fashion	_____	particular
ferment	_____	escape
figment	_____	lighten
finicky	_____	imagined thing
fitfully	_____	wreckage
flaccid	_____	vain
flagrant	_____	limp
flee	_____	open
flourish	_____	shape
foment	_____	unexpected
force	_____	provoke
fortuitous	_____	thrive
fragments	_____	confusion
frequent	_____	habitual
fresh	_____	power
futile	_____	restlessly

G

galvanise	_____	contorted
gauge	_____	estimate
genial	_____	foundation
genuinely	_____	free
gnarled	_____	friendly
gradually	_____	indisputably
grasp	_____	rotate
gratuitous	_____	seize
grave	_____	solemn
groundwork	_____	steadily
gyrate	_____	stir up

H

hazardous	_____	break
heinous	_____	dangerous
hiatus	_____	linger
hinder	_____	moist
hoard	_____	obstruct

homage	_____	put aside
hover	_____	respect
humid	_____	terrible

I

image	_____	about to happen
imminent	_____	at first
impact	_____	awful
inedible	_____	case in point
inevitable	_____	endless
infallible	_____	influence
infernal	_____	intrude
inherent	_____	natural
initially	_____	overwhelm
instance	_____	perfect
instantly	_____	picture
intelligible	_____	priceless
interminable	_____	protest vehemently
interrupt	_____	right away
intimidate	_____	roaming
inundate	_____	threaten
invaluable	_____	understandable
inveigh	_____	unpalatable
itinerant	_____	unstoppable

J

jaded	_____	acceptable
jaunty	_____	authority
jeer	_____	funny
jeopardise	_____	intersection
jilt	_____	laugh at
jocular	_____	lively
jubilant	_____	point in time
judicious	_____	put at risk
junction	_____	put next to
juncture	_____	split up with
jurisdiction	_____	thrilled
justified	_____	tired
juvenile	_____	wise
juxtapose	_____	young

K

kaleidoscope	_____	complain persistently
keen	_____	hill
kickstart	_____	incite
kindle	_____	relationship
kinship	_____	reputation
knell	_____	series of changing phases
knoll	_____	set in motion
knowingly	_____	sharp
kudos	_____	signal of disaster
kvetch	_____	with intent

L

lavish	_____	absurd
leach	_____	agile
lead	_____	clear
level	_____	defame
levity	_____	direct
liability	_____	enraged
libel	_____	fertile
likely	_____	flat
lithe	_____	light-heartedness
livid	_____	mournful
lucid	_____	plentiful
ludicrous	_____	prone
lugubrious	_____	responsibility
luxuriant	_____	trickle

M

main	_____	average
mandatory	_____	bewildered
manifest	_____	compulsory
mask	_____	countless
maximum	_____	disguise
mediocre	_____	dull
menial	_____	environment
mercurial	_____	key
merely	_____	movable
milieu	_____	reasonable
mobile	_____	reproduction
model	_____	routine
moderate	_____	show
monotonous	_____	simply
mundane	_____	tedious
myriad	_____	utmost
mystified	_____	volatile

N

negligent	_____	agile
negligible	_____	cancel out
nicety	_____	careless
nimble	_____	idea
nondescript	_____	infamous
notion	_____	insignificant
notorious	_____	irritation
nourish	_____	nurture
nuance	_____	ordinary
nuisance	_____	small point
nullify	_____	tone

O

objective	_____	appropriate
obsolescent	_____	behind time
obsolete	_____	boding evil
obtrusive	_____	clear
obviate	_____	falling into disuse

obvious	insult
offend	no longer in use
offer	prevent
ominous	suggest
opportune	tremendous
overdue	unmistakable
overwhelming	unprejudiced

P

particularly	assumed role
penetrating	chiefly
perfunctory	code
peripheral	corrective
permanent	credible
persecute	crucial
persona	densely inhabited
perspective	dilemma
pertinent	discriminate against
phenomenal	earlier
phenomenon	exceptionally
pioneer	excess
pivotal	extraordinary
plausible	inflame
plethora	insightful
pocket	lasting
populous	lead the way
precious	major
predicament	minor
prerequisite	observable fact
previous	pledge
primarily	primitive
primordial	put on trial
princely	relevant
principal	requirement
principle	steal
pristine	substantial
promise	unspoilt
prosecute	unthinking
provoke	valuable
punitive	viewpoint

Q

quash	defeat
querulous	irritable
quiescent	perfect example
quintessence	quiet

R

range	adversary
readily	distant
recede	flexible
recoup	get back
refurbish	habitually
regularly	harshness

reign	_____	historical object
relic	_____	loaded
remote	_____	move away
reputation	_____	promptly
resilient	_____	relief
respite	_____	restore
retrieve	_____	standing
rich	_____	take back
rigour	_____	time in power
rival	_____	variety

S

sanction	_____	ample
scarcely	_____	cover
secret	_____	discard
seep	_____	encourage
senseless	_____	faithful
shear	_____	hold up
shed	_____	important
sheer	_____	indicate
shroud	_____	inspiring
significant	_____	keep up
signify	_____	leak
slacken	_____	lean
slender	_____	loud
spectator	_____	methodically
spur	_____	only just
squander	_____	permission
staunch	_____	relax
stealthily	_____	ridiculous
stigma	_____	rigorous
stipulate	_____	secret
strident	_____	shame
stringent	_____	shave
sublime	_____	silently
sufficient	_____	specify
support	_____	steep
surreptitious	_____	undisclosed
sustain	_____	viewer
systematically	_____	waste

T

tacit	_____	agonising
tamper	_____	complete
tardy	_____	complex
tedious	_____	curve
tend	_____	dreary
titillate	_____	gush
torpid	_____	hot
torrent	_____	interfere
torrid	_____	lazy
tortuous	_____	look after
torturous	_____	pass through
total	_____	set off

trace	_____	sign
traverse	_____	sluggish
trigger	_____	thrill
triumphant	_____	unspoken
turn	_____	victorious

U

ulterior	_____	awkward
unanimous	_____	disturbance
uncompromising	_____	exhort
unconscionable	_____	first-time
underlying	_____	hidden
ungainly	_____	make use of
universal	_____	modest
unobtrusive	_____	premature
unprecedented	_____	primary
unrequited	_____	rigid
untimely	_____	undivided
unwary	_____	unreturned
upheaval	_____	unscrupulous
urge	_____	unsuspecting
utilise	_____	worldwide

V

vacuous	_____	blank
vagrant	_____	border
valiant	_____	defenceless
veneer	_____	difficulties
verge	_____	energy
verify	_____	greedy
verve	_____	heroic
vestige	_____	neighbourhood
vicarious	_____	prove
vicinity	_____	shocking
vicissitudes	_____	surface
vigilant	_____	trace
voracious	_____	wandering
vulnerable	_____	watchful

W

wacky	_____	amazing
waif	_____	anger
waive	_____	complain
watershed	_____	connect
weld	_____	crafty
wheedle	_____	droop
whine	_____	endure
wholesome	_____	fragment
will	_____	give up
wilt	_____	humour
wily	_____	hurt
wisp	_____	mad
wit	_____	nourishing
withstand	_____	persuade

wondrous	_____	resolve
wound	_____	soul
wrath	_____	turning point

Y

yank	_____	produce
yarn	_____	pull
yield	_____	tall story

Z

zany	_____	appetite
zealous	_____	crazy
zenith	_____	keen
zest	_____	peak

Answers (Part 1 And Part 2)

Unit 1

1. protested
2. objected
3. implored
4. acknowledged
5. declared
6. contended
7. refuted
8. pronounced
9. suggested
10. announced
11. claimed
12. confessed
13. proclaimed
14. reiterated
15. rejoined
16. asserted
17. swore
18. countered
19. stressed
20. reasoned
21. affirmed
22. lamented
23. insisted
24. snorted
25. muttered
26. conceded
27. demanded
28. retorted
29. begged
30. complained

Unit 2

1. unpredictable, capricious, inconsistent
2. indecisive, irresolute, hesitant
3. temperamental, mercurial, volatile
4. inscrutable, mysterious, unfathomable
5. effusive, demonstrative, unrestrained
6. candid, frank, outspoken
7. vindictive, vengeful, malicious
8. insincere, superficial, glib

Unit 3

1. (b)
2. (d)
3. (d)
4. (a)
5. (c)
6. (a)
7. (b)
8. (d)
9. (a)
10. (a)
11. (c)
12. (a)
13. (c)
14. (d)
15. (b)
16. (b)
17. (c)
18. (b)
19. (d)
20. (c)

Unit 4

A:
1. trimmed
2. slashed
3. dissecting
4. splitting
5. severed/severs
6. carved
7. chop
8. hacked/hacks
9. sliced/slices
10. snipped
11. notched
12. hewed/hews
13. lacerated
14. slit

B:
1. j, n
2. a
3. m
4. k
5. i
6. o
7. g
8. c
9. l
10. h
11. b
12. e
13. d
14. f

'Carve' has two meanings: 'make something by cutting into the surface' or 'cut thin slices from a large piece of meat'.

Unit 5

A:
1. a b b r e v i a t e d
2. a b r i d g e d
3. a b r u p t
4. b r i s k
5. b r u s q u e
6. c o n c i s e
7. c o n d e n s e d
8. c r i s p
9. c u r t
10. e c o n o m i c a l

11. `e p i g r a m m a t i c`

12. `i n c i s i v e`

13. `l a c o n i c`

14. `m o n o s y l l a b i c`

15. `p i t h y`

16. `p o i n t e d`

17. `s u c c i n c t`

18. `s u m m a r i s e d`

19. `t a c i t u r n`

20. `t e r s e`

21. `t r e n c h a n t`

22. `t r u n c a t e d`

B:
1. economical
2. pithy
3. taciturn
4. terse
5. brusque
6. incisive
7. abridged
8. summarised
9. succinct
10. epigrammatic

Unit 6

1. soft-hearted
2. feather-brained
3. hot-headed
4. bare-footed, cross-legged
5. cold-blooded
6. tight-fisted
7. foul-mouthed
8. pot-bellied
9. narrow-minded
10. empty-handed
11. high-handed
12. red-faced, red-handed
13. big-headed
14. bald-faced
15. bare-chested

Unit 7

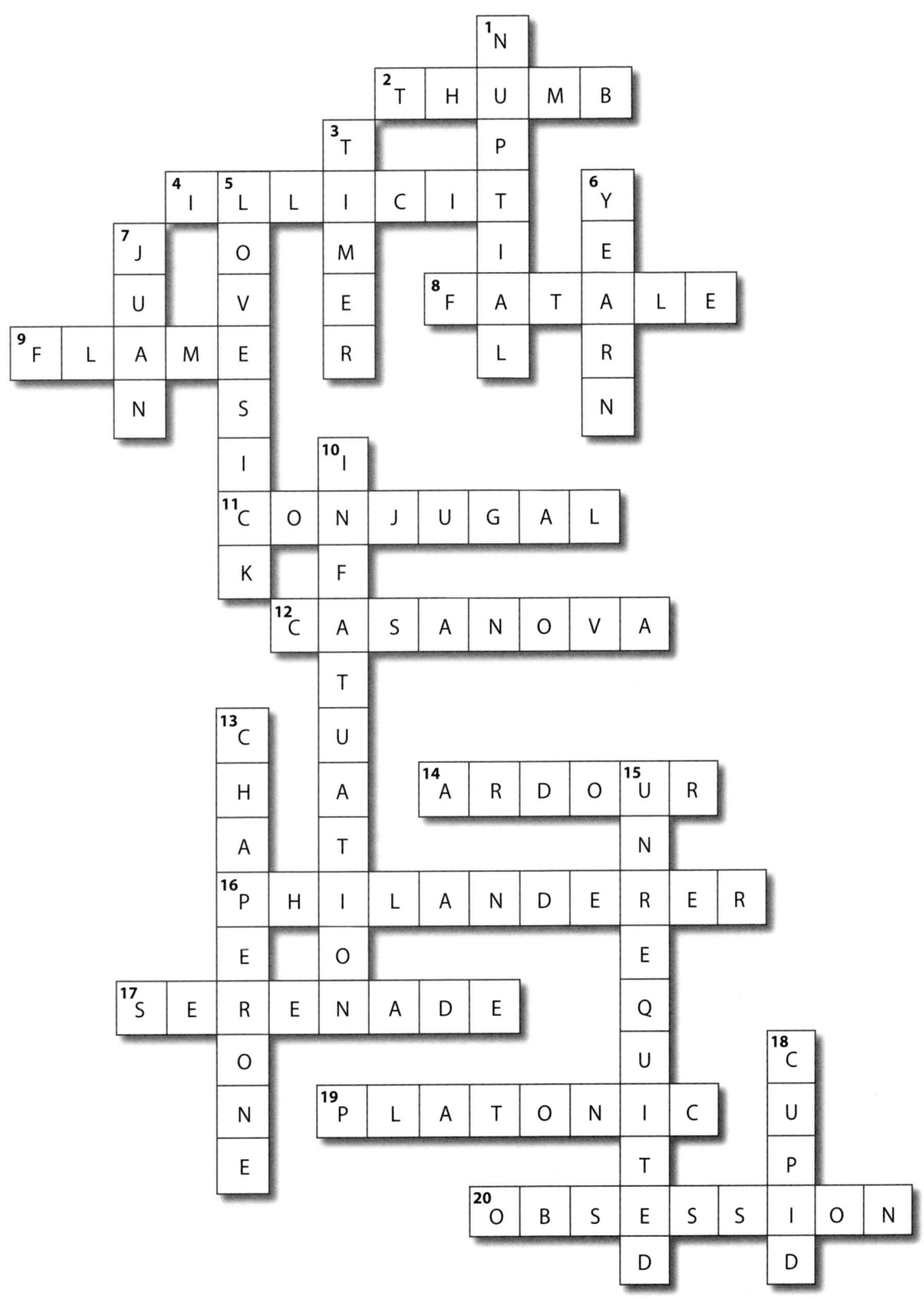

Unit 8

1. blasted
2. castigated
3. lambasted
4. vilified
5. pilloried
6. rebuked
7. berated
8. chided
9. admonished
10. reproved
11. reprimanded
12. censured
13. chastised
14. harangued

Unit 9

1. balaclava
2. beret
3. bandana
4. parka
5. poncho
6. toga
7. cravat
8. cummerbund
9. overalls
10. cardigan
11. waistcoat
12. vest
13. tuxedo
14. shawl

Unit 10

Hardworking
diligent
sedulous
assiduous
industrious
persevering
studious
indefatigable
painstaking
unflagging
unrelenting

Lazy
slothful
indolent
lackadaisical
lethargic
unproductive
apathetic
languid
shiftless
languorous
sluggish
laid-back
complacent
torpid
idle

Proud
overbearing
supercilious
lofty
disdainful
cocky
egotistical
high-handed
imperious
pompous
pretentious
self-important
vainglorious
cavalier
presumptuous

Humble
unpretentious
modest
lowly
obsequious
self-effacing
unobtrusive
submissive
commonplace
insignificant
obscure
servile
unassuming
menial
deferential

Unit 11

A:
1. colony
2. shrewdness
3. pace
4. sloth
5. army
6. clowder
7. clutter
8. drove
9. peep
10. murder
11. cowardice
12. kennel
13. dule
14. raft
15. paddling
16. convocation
17. business
18. skulk
19. gaggle
20. skein
21. trip
22. charm
23. cloud
24. leash
25. husk
26. cast
27. siege
28. drift
29. mute
30. cluster
31. smack
32. mob
33. kindle
34. deceit
35. exaltation
36. leap
37. pride
38. plague
39. labour
40. barrel
41. watch
42. parliament
43. team
44. company
45. covey
46. ostentation
47. rye
48. congregation
49. string
50. run
51. field
52. unkindness
53. crash
54. building
55. pod
56. host
57. dray
58. murmuration
59. mustering
60. knot
61. hover
62. rafter
63. pitying
64. bale
65. nest
66. gam
67. destruction
68. rout
69. descent

B:
1. n
2. d
3. h
4. g
5. o
6. i
7. p
8. m
9. r
10. c
11. k
12. q
13. t
14. a
15. s
16. l
17. e
18. u
19. f
20. v
21. b
22. j

Unit 12

WHITE
chalky water
creamy paper
ivory cloth
milky skin
pearly teeth
snow-white shoes

BLACK
ebony skirt
inky night
jet-black hair
pitch-black sky
pitchy room
raven hair
sable skies

GREY
ashen face
ashy cheeks
charcoal skin
cinerous dusk
hoary beard
pepper-and-salt
    complexion
silvery-grey car
slate-grey floor
smoky eyes
steel-grey door

BROWN
auburn hair
beige envelope
bronzed shoulders
chestnut table
chocolate-brown suit
hazel eyes
khaki pants
mahogany wardrobe
mustard-coloured cravat
ochre desk
russet evening
sepia-toned photograph
tawny shirt

PURPLE
lavender curtain
lilac petticoat
mauve sweater
tyrian purple nails
violet eyeshadow

BLUE
aquamarine light
azure sky
cerulean eyeliner
cobalt blue
    Volkswagon
indigo belt
navy blue jeans
prussian blouse
royal blue shorts
sapphire water
turquoise eyes

RED
burgundy lips
carroty cheeks
coral red fingernails
crimson sunrise
maroon miniskirt
rose-coloured paper
ruby-red dress
scarlet silk
vermilion tassels
wine-red gloves

GREEN
emerald bracken
lime print
olive eyes
verdant garden
viridescent eyeshadow

YELLOW
blond hair
butter-coloured hat
cadmium yellow tie
chrome yellow
    brightness
flaxen skin
golden sunrise
saffron jacket
sandy hair

ORANGE
amber headlights
apricot scarf
coppery skin
ginger eyebrows
ochreous sunlight
tangerine morning

A green-eyed monster is a jealous person. 'Being in the pink' means to be feeling fit while 'seeing red' means becoming suddenly angry and losing one's self-control. A purple passage is a piece of writing which is 'overdone' or unnecessarily elaborate.

Unit 13

A: 1.   a. spectre
           b. spirit
           c. sprite
           d. spook
    2.   a. phantom
           b. bogeyman
           c. apparition
           d. ghoul
           e. wraith
    3.   paranormal phenomena
    4.   a. iii
           b. i
           c. iv
           d. ii

B: 1.   dead to the world
    2.   graveyard shift
    3.   ghost town
    4.   ghost of a chance
    5.   done to death
    6.   ghostwrites/ghosts
    7.   gave up the ghost
    8.   dead set
    9.   dead man's switch
    10. nail in his coffin

Unit 14

A:
1. to
2. off
3. in
4. in
5. on
6. in
7. out
8. off
9. off
10. over

B:

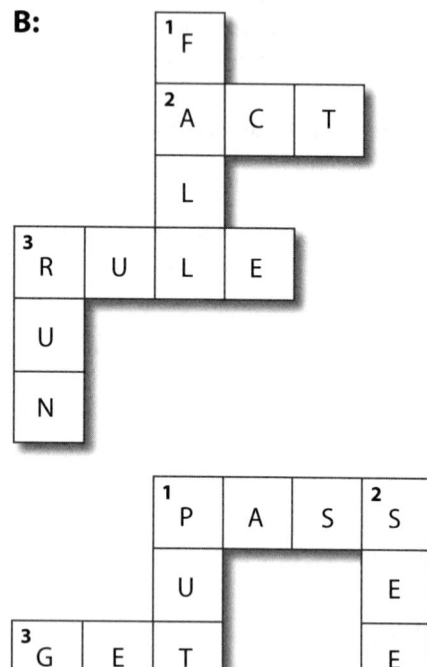

C:
1. done away with
2. put up with
3. feel up to
4. getting on for
5. go in for
6. fallen out with
7. do out of
8. go back on

Unit 15

Good	Bad
benevolent	abysmal
bona fide	apocryphal
consummate	baleful
immaculate	debauched
impartial	detrimental
impeccable	diabolical
judicious	duplicitous
magnanimous	egregious
meritorious	flagrant
principled	fraudulent
scrupulous	heinous
seraphic	infernal
stupendous	insidious
sublime	malevolent

Good	Bad
unparalleled	nefarious
veracious	odious

Unit 16

Better an ugly face than an ugly mind. (James Ellis)

Unit 17

A:
1. pageboy
2. frizz
3. fringe
4. Afro
5. bouffant
6. mohawk
7. dreadlocks
8. pompadour
9. spikes

B:
1. coiffure
2. crew cut
3. tousled
4. receding hairline
5. clean-cut
6. mane
7. jarhead or skinhead
8. wave
9. bob
10. braid

Unit 18

Mrs Malaprop meant to say 'expose' instead of 'explode' and 'obliterate' instead of 'illiterate'.

elected — selected
suppressed — impressed
expansive — expensive
ravenous — ravishing
illegible — eligible
conservationist — conversationalist
constipation — consternation
antidotes — anecdotes
putrefied — petrified
effluent — affluent
infest — invest
auspicious — officious
abdominal — abominable

Unit 19

A: hangover
stand-in
layout
handover
breakout
shakeup
turn-on
setback
cover-up
lie-in
standup
outlay
hold-up
breakthrough
shakedown
write-up
set-up

walkout
drive-in
fallout
layoff
turnover
break-in
turnout
write-off
onset
cutback
fallback
handout
outbreak
crackdown
outset
drawback

B:
1. layoffs
2. crackdown
3. fallback
4. fallout
5. handout
6. write-up
7. shakedown
8. turnout
9. breakout
10. breakthrough
11. onset
12. outset
13. layout
14. outlay

Unit 20

1. episodic
2. cursory
3. ephemeral
4. evanescent
5. momentary
6. passing
7. fleeting
8. short-lived
9. transient
10. fugacious
11. transitory
12. impermanent
13. fugitive
14. temporal
15. interim

Unit 21

1. P R O S R A I H A C
prosaic

2. T P E D R E S W T R I A N
pedestrian

3. M A T U N D A T N E
mundane

4. E R A R X T H T B O U N D
earthbound

5. B A N O A T L A
banal

6. R V A I C U E O U S
vacuous

7. I T N E A N B E
inane

8. I N A G E N S U D O U S
ingenuous

9. T Q U X O T I R D I A N
quotidian

10. T E R I O T E R
trite

11. O P L E G O B E I A N
plebeian

12. P A T R O E C H I D A L
parochial

13. S O A P O U R I F I C A
soporific

14. G U E I L E L E S O S M
guileless

15. M E A L D I U O C R E
mediocre

Unit 22

A:
1. reticulated
2. orbicular
3. tubular
4. funnel
5. elliptic
6. conical
7. prism
8. tessellated
9. serrated
10. cuneate
11. spiral
12. toothed
13. hexagonal
14. scallop
15. trifurcated
16. pretzel
17. bulbous
18. corrugated

B:
1. cordate
2. acicular
3. whorl
4. furrowed
5. amorphous
6. undulating
7. trihedral
8. protuberant
9. campanulate
10. bacillary
11. stellate
12. palmate

Unit 23

1. eternal
2. immutable
3. immortal
4. perpetual
5. interminable
6. perennial
7. infinite
8. incessant
9. relentless
10. unceasing
11. unflagging
12. amaranthine
13. timeless
14. prolonged
15. ageless

Unit 24

A:
1. deplored
2. decried
3. derided
4. condemned
5. lambasted
6. denounced
7. belittle
8. bemoaned
9. disparaged
10. ridiculed
11. maligned
12. rapped
13. denigrated
14. taunted
15. fulminated
16. slammed
17. panned
18. inveighed
19. humiliated
20. faulted

B:

To disapprove or blame	To condemn or criticise abusively	To clear from blame
censure	curse	absolve
deprecate	excoriate	acquit
indict	execrate	exculpate
reproach	revile	exonerate
reprobate	vituperate	vindicate

C: remonstrate: protest, argue

Unit 25

1. anagram — a word or phrase formed by changing the sequence of letters of another — 'Desperation' = 'A rope ends it'

2. spoonerism — a word or phrase in which the letters or syllables get swapped — 'A lack of pies' = 'A pack of lies'

3. malapropism — misuse of a word in place of one that sounds like it, often with amusing results — 'He is the very pineapple of politeness!'

4. palindrome — a word or phrase that reads the same forwards and backwards — 'Never odd or even'

5. mnemonic — a sentence that is supposed to help one remember — 'V I Boys Get Your Orange Ready!' = The colours of the rainbow (Violet, Indigo, Blue, Green, Yellow, Orange, Red)

6.	acronym	a word formed from the first letters of another word	'WYSIWYG'= What you see is what you get
7.	euphemism	a milder expression instead of a harsh or offensive one	'sanitation worker' = 'garbage man'
8.	onomatopoeia	the use of words that imitate sounds	'The quick sharp scratch and blue spurt of a lighted match'
9.	pangram	a sentence that uses every letter of the alphabet	'The quick brown fox jumps over the lazy dog.'
10.	oxymoron	a combination of contradictory words	'genuine imitation' and 'original copies'
11.	jargon	the specialised or technical expressions of a particular field or profession	'If you intend to use PHP for command line scripting, you always need the command line executable.'
12.	epigram	a witty, often paradoxical remark	'Life is far too important a thing ever to talk seriously about.'

Unit 26

A:
1. cut and run
2. wine and dine
3. law and order
4. nuts and bolts
5. down and out
6. sixes and sevens
7. blood and thunder
8. nook and cranny
9. thick and thin
10. prim and proper
11. spick and span
12. rack and ruin

B:
1. beck and call
2. chalk and cheese
3. cut and paste
4. hue and cry
5. up and about
6. touch and go
7. thick and fast
8. fair and square
9. sick and tired
10. sink or swim
11. all or nothing
12. sooner or later

C: 'Give-and-take' means 'willingness to make compromises'. For a marriage to work, there has to be some give-and-take. 'Give or take' means 'more or less' or 'approximately'. There were 300 people at the seminar, give or take a few.

Unit 27

A:
1. d
2. h
3. i
4. b
5. a
6. j
7. e
8. g
9. f
10. c

B:
1. flabbergasted
2. embellishment
3. tintinnabulation
4. augmentation
5. predilection
6. gobbledygook
7. ineffable
8. pusillanimous
9. prevarication
10. serendipitous

Unit 28

A:

B:
1. lug
2. lax
3. ply
4. ilk
5. ebb
6. yen
7. rig
8. woo

Unit 29

A:

Adjectives	Nouns
audacious	audacity
bold	boldness
brave	bravery
chivalrous	chivalry
daring	daringness
dauntless	dauntlessness
defiant	defiance
doughty	doughtiness
fearless	fearlessness
gallant	gallantry
gritty	grit
hardy	hardiness
heroic	heroism
indomitable	indomitability
intrepid	intrepidity
invincible	invincibility
lion-hearted	lion-heartedness
mettlesome	mettle
plucky	pluckiness
pugnacious	pugnacity
resolute	resoluteness
spunky	spunk
stalwart	stalwartness
stouthearted	stoutheartedness
temerarious	temerity
tenacious	tenacity
undaunted	undauntedness
valiant	valiance
venturesome	venturesomeness

B:
1. Don Quixote (the idealistic hero of the satirical chivalric romance by Miguel de Cervantes)
2. daredevil
3. Amazon (a tall, aggressive and strong-willed woman; in classical legend the Amazons were a tribe of warrior women)
4. Joan of Arc (French military leader and heroine)
5. David (the second king of Judah and Israel; according to the Bible, he slew the Philistine giant, Goliath, and succeeded Saul as king)
6. Bayard (French military hero known for his fearlessness and chivalry)
7. paladin (a strong supporter or defender of a cause)
8. Robin Hood (legendary English outlaw of the 12th century, known for his courage, chivalry and practice of robbing the rich to help the poor)

Unit 30

1.

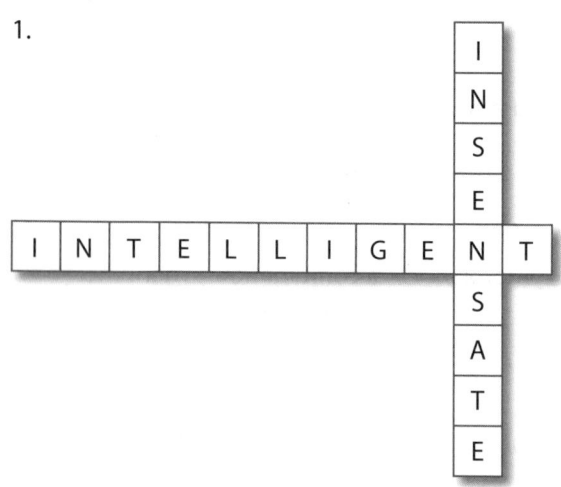

2.

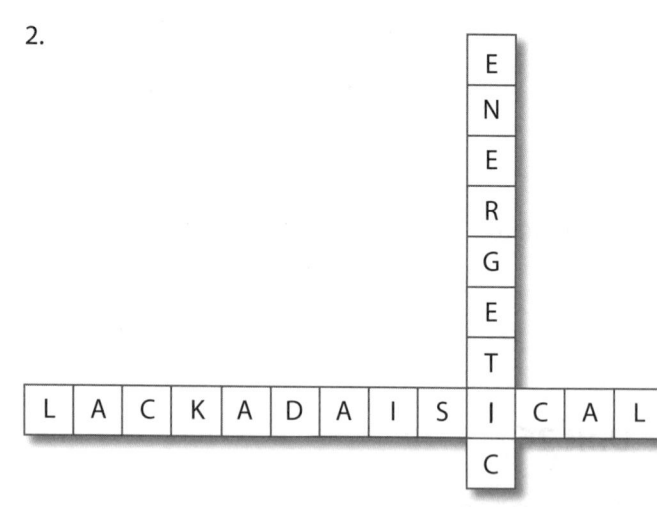

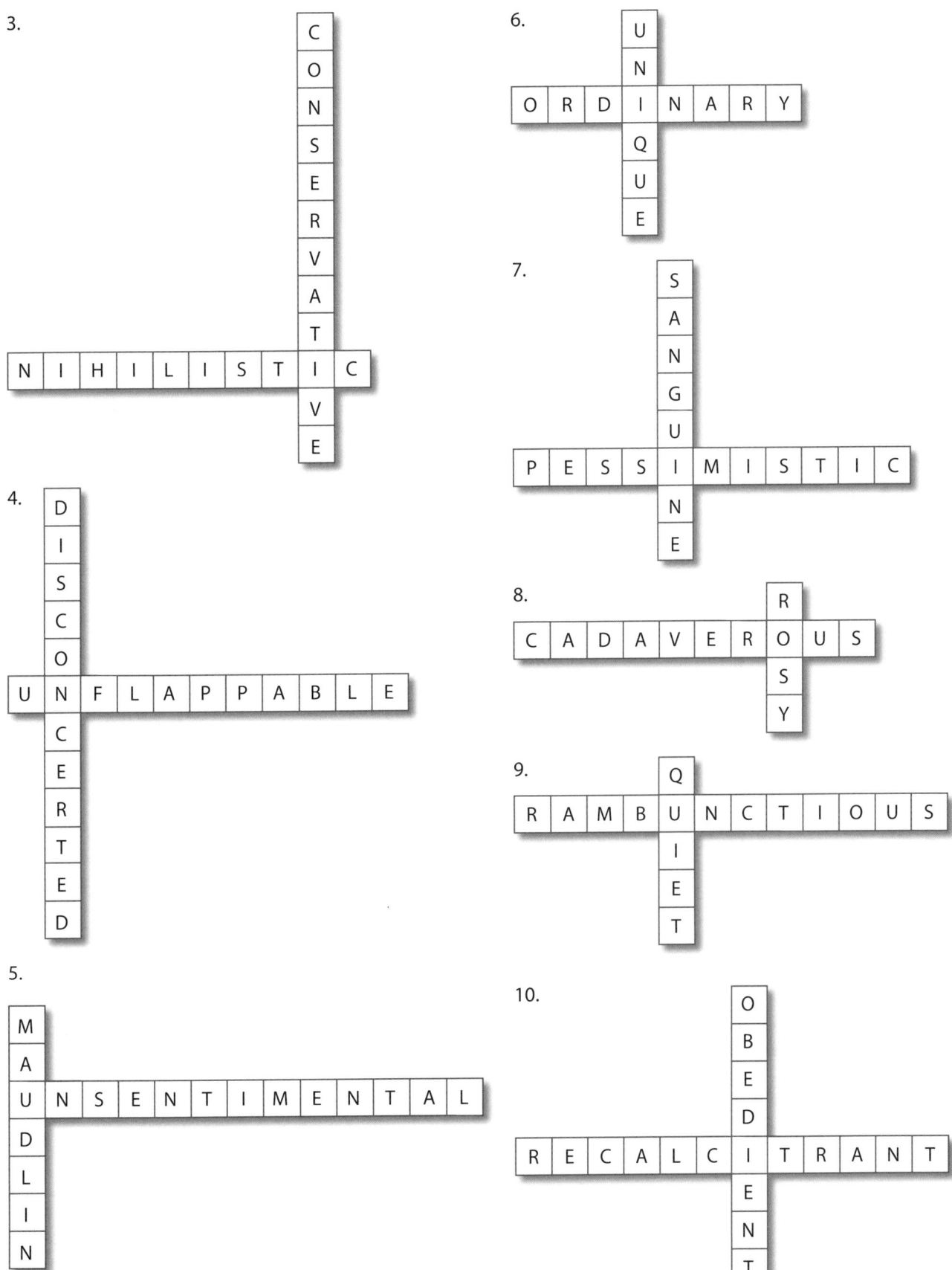

3.

C
O
N
S
E
R
V
A
T
N I H I L I S T I C
V
E

6.

U
N
O R D I N A R Y
Q
U
E

7.

S
A
N
G
U
P E S S I M I S T I C
N
E

4.

D
I
S
C
O
U N F L A P P A B L E
C
E
R
T
E
D

8.

R
C A D A V E R O U S
S
Y

9.

Q
R A M B U N C T I O U S
I
E
T

5.

M
A
U N S E N T I M E N T A L
D
L
I
N

10.

O
B
E
D
R E C A L C I T R A N T
E
N
T

11.

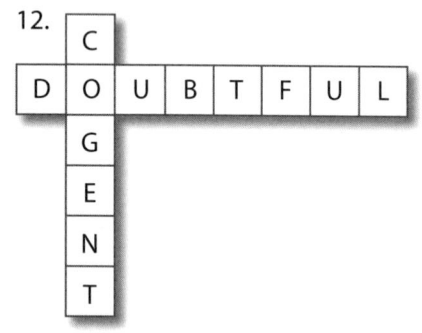

12.

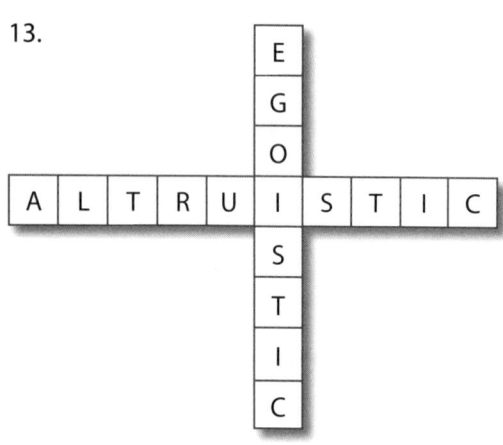

13.

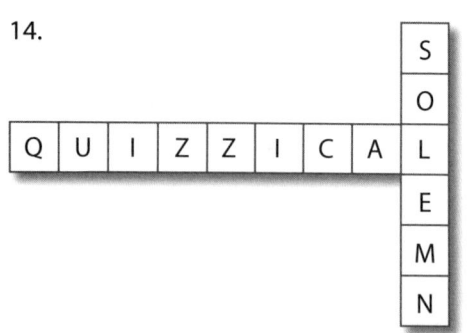

14.

15.

Unit 31

A:
1. garnet
2. amethyst
3. aquamarine
4. diamond
5. emerald
6. pearl
7. ruby
8. peridot
9. sapphire
10. opal
11. citrine
12. turquoise

B:
1. ruby-red, pearly white
2. emerald, aquamarine, turquoise (in any order)
3. pearls
4. diamond

Unit 32

A:
1. c   3. i   5. e   7. b   9. d
2. j   4. f   6. h   8. a   10. g

B:
1. Hypnosis
2. Pandora's box
3. mnemonic
4. tantalising
5. narcissistic
6. promethean
7. Midas touch
8. nemesis
9. siren
10. gorgon

Unit 33

A:
1. well-documented
2. exhaustive
3. searching
4. cogent
5. incisive
6. meticulous
7. accurate
8. painstaking
9. consummate
10. unequivocal

Unit 34

A:

1.						H	E	R	B	A	L	I	S	T	
2.			D	E	T	E	C	T	I	O	N				
3.					P	R	O	T	A	G	O	N	I	S	T
4.						C	O	U	R	T	R	O	O	M	
5.	A	M	A	T	E	U	R								
6.			F	O	I	L									
7.			F	O	R	E	N	S	I	C					
8.			P	E	R	P	E	T	R	A	T	O	R		
9.				M	O	T	I	V	E						
10.				A	L	I	B	I							
11.				T	R	U	S	T							
12.				W	H	O	D	U	N	N	I	T			
13.					T	W	I	S	T						

B: The fictional detective is Hercule Poirot and the writer was Agatha Christie. Hercule Poirot appeared in two of her most famous stories, *Death on the Nile* and *Murder on the Orient Express*.

Unit 35

A: infotainment (information + entertainment)
infomercial (information + commercial)
edutainment (education + entertainment)
advertorial (advertising + editorial)
jazzercise (jazz + exercise)
buffeteria (buffet + cafeteria)
camcorder (camera + recorder)
faction (fact + fiction)
Rolodex (rolling + index)
netizen (Internet + citizen)
biopic (biography + picture)
emoticon (emotion + icon)
sitcom (situation + comedy)
animatronics (animation + electronics)
docudrama (documentary + drama)
smog (smoke + fog)
brunch (breakfast + lunch)
Pictionary (picture + dictionary)
simulcast (simultaneous + broadcast)
cyborg (cybernetic + organism)

B:
1. animatronics
2. buffeteria
3. camcorder
4. netizens
5. docudrama
6. Rolodex
7. jazzercise
8. emoticons
9. sitcom
10. Pictionary

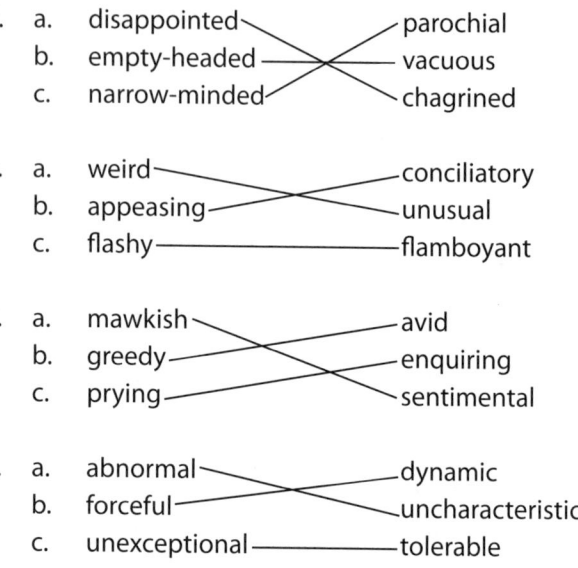

5. a. disappointed — chagrined
   b. empty-headed — vacuous
   c. narrow-minded — parochial

6. a. weird — unusual
   b. appeasing — conciliatory
   c. flashy — flamboyant

7. a. mawkish — sentimental
   b. greedy — avid
   c. prying — enquiring

8. a. abnormal — uncharacteristic
   b. forceful — dynamic
   c. unexceptional — tolerable

Unit 36

1. a. lazy — languorous
   b. moody — mercurial
   c. ordinary — banal

2. a. disrespectful — irreverent
   b. sarcastic — ironic
   c. meddlesome — officious

3. a. embittered — acrid
   b. argumentative — litigious
   c. threatening — intimidating

4. a. insensitive — stolid
   b. reckless — audacious
   c. interfering — inquisitive

Unit 37

A:

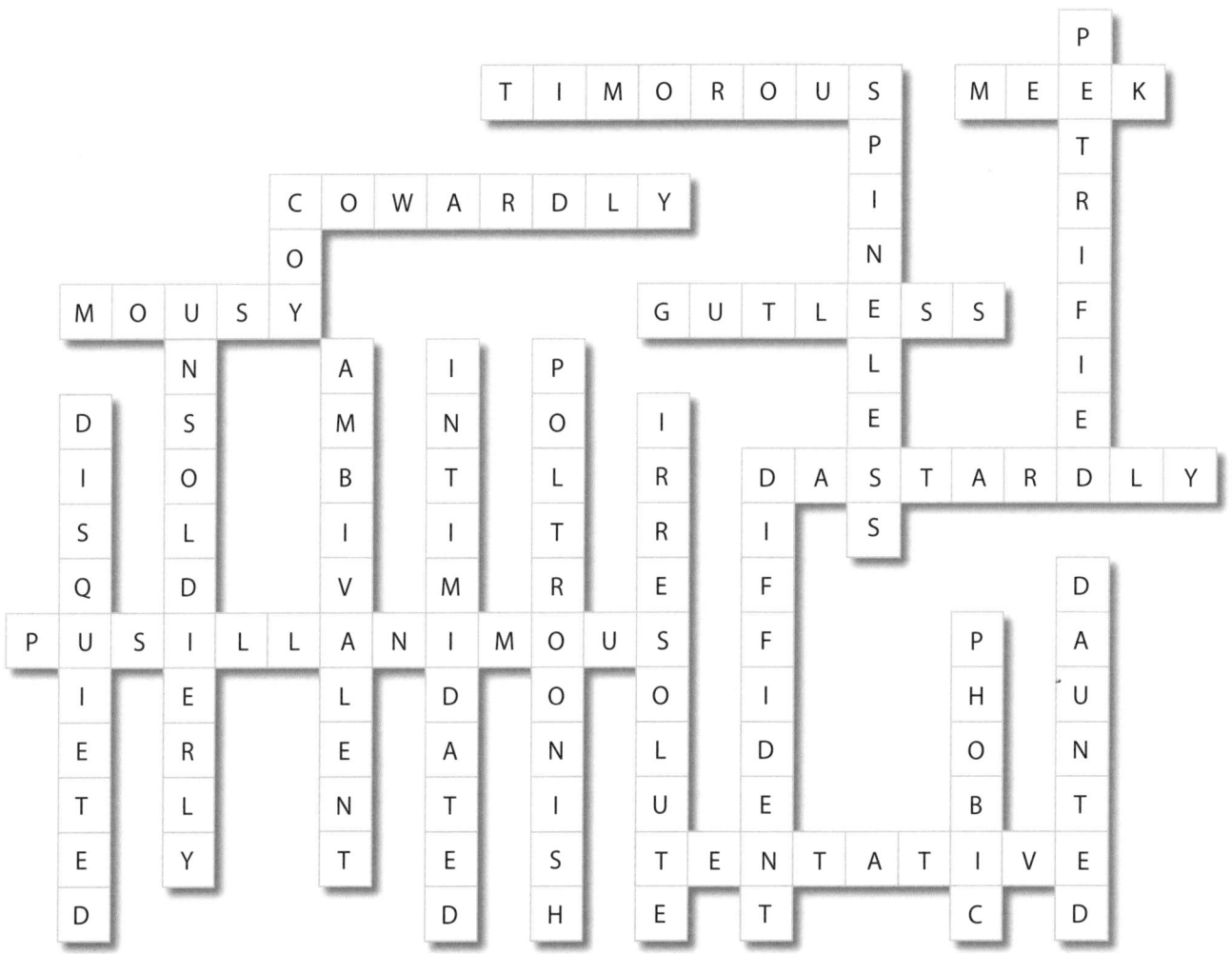

Unit 38

Synonyms of 'timid':

1. ambivalent
2. cowardly
3. coy
4. dastardly
5. daunted
6. diffident
7. disquieted
8. gutless
9. intimidated
10. irresolute
11. meek
12. mousy
13. petrified
14. phobic
15. poltroonish
16. pusillanimous
17. spineless
18. tentative
19. timorous
20. unsoldierly

A poltroon is an old name for a coward.

Unit 39

11 SHAPELY

10 RAVISHING

9 SCENIC

8 STRIKING

7 GLAMOROUS

6 RESPLENDENT

5 ORNAMENTAL

4 STUNNING

3 EXQUISITE

2 GORGEOUS

1 AESTHETIC

'Picturesque' means scenic.

Unit 40

(Accept other suitable words or expressions.)
2. He lied.
3. He was careless.
4. He's fat and old.
5. We had to have our Labrador killed.
6. In the middle of the test I had to go to the toilet.
7. You were drunk last evening after three cans of beer.
8. Your product is badly made.
9. There are many people who are poor and need jobs in the country.
10. The tour guide advised us to avoid the dangerous parts of the town.
11. You've been insensitive.
12. The discussions have been a waste of time.
13. His coat was very shabby.
14. The old man died last night.
15. Old people need not pay the entrance fees to the zoo.
16. He's jobless.
17. The supervisor dismissed him because he was lazy.
18. The lieutenant could not explain the civilian deaths caused by the military action.
19. There are many poor people who need our help.
20. After a series of failures, she's beginning to doubt herself.

Unit 41

1. all fingers and thumbs
2. a cold fish
3. a chip off the old block
4. a fairweather friend
5. a memory like a sieve
6. a flash in the pan
7. wet behind the ears
8. a mover and shaker
9. a kindred spirit
10. head in the clouds
11. feet on the ground
12. a hard nut to crack
13. constitution of an ox
14. a shrinking violet

Unit 42

1. It is easier to teach a *homogeneous* class.
2. When you write an essay for the exam, make sure that you do not introduce *extraneous/superfluous* material.
3. Her vivacity and high spirits are *infectious*.
4. The boys are especially *boisterous* today.
5. Rock climbing in this part of the world can be dangerous because of the *capricious* weather.
6. I can't stand that man because he is *officious*.
7. I know the sea looks peaceful and calm now, but it can be *treacherous*.
8. The audience broke into *spontaneous* applause as the dance came to an end.
9. I've always thought that it must be a useful skill to have — being *ambidextrous*.
10. The dress that Cheryl wore at the prom was *outrageous* — I'm surprised her mother allowed her to wear it!
11. The taxi driver intentionally took a more *circuitous/tortuous* route.
12. Several *ominous* cracks began to appear in the wall.
13. I'm sure you will find her an excellent employee: hardworking and *conscientious*.
14. I found the views written in the editorial *ambiguous*.

Unit 43

A: **Healthy:** robust, vigorous, strapping, hardy, blooming, flourishing, virile, athletic, a clean bill of health, in rude health, in the pink

Sick: ailing, infirm, delicate, feeble, emaciated, malnourished, wan, debilitated, indisposed, bedridden, at death's door, under the weather, go under the knife

B:
1. contagion
2. relapse
3. hypertension
4. haemorrhage
5. panacea
6. hypochondriac
7. apoplexy
8. congenital
9. inflammation
10. Coronary

Unit 44

1. respectful, obsequious
2. articulate, glib
3. trusting, gullible
4. self-reliant, anti-social
5. keen, fanatical
6. broad-minded, permissive
7. meticulous, fussy
8. imaginative, fanciful
9. blunt, frank
10. insincere, tactful
11. helpful, officious
12. laid-back, lackadaisical

Unit 45

A:

1.	b	7.	f	13.	q
2.	g	8.	e	14.	k
3.	d	9.	j	15.	m
4.	c	10.	l	16.	n
5.	h	11.	o	17.	i
6.	a	12.	p		

B:

1.	m	6.	b	10.	d
2.	h	7.	a	11.	j
3.	e	8.	c	12.	g
4.	i	9.	f	13.	k
5.	l				

Unit 47

1. robot
2. robotics
3. artificial intelligence
4. android
5. cyborg
6. nanotechnology
7. cyberspace
8. teleportation
9. cloning
10. terraforming
11. extraterrestrial
12. cryonics
13. parallel universe
14. time loop
15. time travel
16. wormhole

Unit 48

A:
1. IBM — International Business Machines (Corporation) (ab)
2. scuba — Self-Contained Underwater Breathing Apparatus (ac)
3. HTML — HyperText Markup Language (ab)
4. POW — Prisoner of War (ab)
5. LASIK — Laser-Assisted In Situ Keratomileusis (ac)
6. UNICEF — United Nations International Children's Emergency Fund (now United Nations Children's Fund) (ac)
7. ASEAN — Association of Southeast Asian Nations (ac)
8. SMS — Short Message Service (ab)
9. SARS — Severe Acute Respiratory Syndrome (ac)
10. CNN — Cable News Network (ab)

TLA stands for 'three-letter acronym' or 'three-letter abbreviation'. You will notice that TLA is itself a TLA! TLC stands for 'tender loving care'.

B: Memorandum to all Project Managers

Please remind your team members that they are not to engage in multi-level marketing activities. The Chief Executive Officer, Mr Sim, has noticed some employees selling tupperware and beauty products during office hours, and has issued a stern statement that everyone is to cease this activity as soon as possible. Please note: Just because Mr Sim's wife comes in once in a while to sell such products doesn't mean that employees can too.

Regards
Sally Sim
Human Resource Manager

C:
1. Absolutely no genetically modified products sold here — d
2. Departing Singapore 0800 Arriving Brisbane 1600 — c
3. *When Death Comes Knocking* (Parental Guidance) 12 midnight — b
4. Some frequently asked questions on cholesterol screening — a

A deejay (DJ) is a disc jockey and a veejay (VJ) is a video jockey. A deejay is someone who introduces or provides commentary for music recordings at a disco or on radio and TV programmes, and a veejay does the same for videotaped programmes, especially music videos. An emcee (MC) is a master of ceremonies, one who acts as a host at a formal event, introducing other speakers, etc.

Unit 49

A: eyes — hooded, piercing, bloodshot
ears — cauliflower, pierced
nose — upturned, aquiline
hair — flyaway, mousy, receding
forehead — lined, furrowed
eyebrows — knitted, pencil-thin
chin — double, cleft
cheeks — hollow, sallow
lips — pursed, full

B:

1. <u>My heart was in my mouth</u> as I watched the fireman try to reach the child on the roof of the building.

2. Her uncharacteristically rude answer caused <u>raised eyebrows</u> in the class.

3. You mustn't resign from your new position just because you are angry at your boss — don't <u>cut your nose to spite your face</u>.

4. We've had <u>our ear to the ground</u> for the last month so that we'll be the first to know if the company is going to be sold.

5. Try not to be intimidated by your new job and your new colleagues — keep <u>your chin up</u>!

6. Remember to <u>keep your hair on</u> when you work with Wally — he'll do his best to rile you and make you lose your cool.

7. The disappointing news that she had failed to enter the university of her choice was a <u>kick in the teeth</u>.

8. When I blurted out at the meeting that it was Steve's fault we couldn't make the deadline, he gave me <u>the evil eye</u>.

9. The poor lived <u>cheek by jowl</u> in run-down tenements on the edge of the city — it's no wonder the epidemic spread so fast there.

10. 'Don't <u>give me any of your lip</u>, young miss!' hissed the librarian when I tried to explain why the books had come crashing down from the shelf.

Unit 50

A:

1. madrigal. The others are religious in nature.
2. bassoon. The others are stringed instruments.
3. harp. The others are brass instruments.
4. viola. The others are woodwind instruments.
5. clarinet. The others are percussion instruments.
6. harpsichord. The others are modern musical players.
7. soprano. The others are classical music compositions.
8. quartet. The others are the different parts in vocal harmony.
9. vocalist. The others are instrumentalists — musicians who perform on a musical instrument.
10. ballad. The others are different genres of music.
11. alto. The others are musical directions as to how to play a piece of music.

12. Picasso. The others were famous musical composers.

B:

1.	orchestra	5.	castanets
2.	pit	6.	synthesiser
3.	genre	7.	plectrum
4.	harmony	8.	bagpipe

Unit 51

1. Bakelite
2. sideburns
3. draconian
4. epicure
5. bowdlerise
6. ritzy
7. bobby
8. paparazzi
9. Peach Melba
10. Lindy Hop
11. namby pamby (Part of the poem reads: 'Namby Pamby's Little Rhimes, Little Jingle, Little Chimes.')
12. Orwellian

Unit 52

1.	h	5.	l	9.	b	13.	e
2.	n	6.	k	10.	d	14.	p
3.	g	7.	o	11.	f	15.	m
4.	i	8.	a	12.	c	16.	j

Unit 53

A: Japan
honcho, origami, ikebana, futon, manga, haiku, aikido, dojo

Russia
bistro, sputnik, borsch, glastnost, perestroika, tundra, cosmonaut, steppe

Germany
delicatessen, hamburger, strudel, dachshund, kindergarten, frankfurter, waltz, poltergeist

France
cuisine, chauffeur, billet-doux, connoisseur, cul-de-sac, chalet, boutique, elite

Italy
pasta, vendetta, fiasco, campanile, caricature, piazza, virtuoso, soprano

B:
1. manga
2. poltergeist
3. strudel
4. cul-de-sac
5. Aikido
6. borsch
7. connoisseur
8. vendetta
9. haiku
10. pasta
11. tundra
12. delicatessen

Unit 54

A:
1. finger in every pie
2. hot potato
3. cream of the crop
4. take with a pinch of salt
5. full of beans
6. chew the fat
7. half-baked
8. stew in one's own juice
9. in hot soup
10. bring home the bacon

B:
1. cream of the crop
2. finger in every pie
3. with a pinch of salt
4. half-baked
5. in hot soup
6. stew in his own juice
7. full of beans
8. hot potato
9. bring home the bacon
10. chew the fat

Unit 55

1. j. Pollyanna. The name of the heroine in a series of books written for children by the American author Eleanor Hodgman Porter.
2. d. Svengali. The name of the hypnotist in George du Maurier's novel, *Trilby*.
3. k. Don Quixote. The hero of Miguel Cervantes' novel of the same name.
4. i. Man Friday (or Girl Friday). A character in *Robinson Crusoe* by Daniel Defoe.
5. f. Lothario. A character in *The Fair Penitent*, a play by Nicholas Rowe.
6. a. Peter Pan. The mischievous hero of J. M. Barrie's play of the same name. Peter Pan is the 'boy who never grew up'.
7. b. Jekyll and Hyde. The protagonist Dr Jekyll, a kind doctor, succeeds in separating himself into two personalities — Dr Hyde is his evil persona. From the book *The Strange Case of Dr Jekyll and Mr Hyde* by Robert Louis Stevenson.
8. e. Shylock. The ruthless Jewish money lender in Shakespeare's *The Merchant of Venice*.
9. g. Mrs Grundy. The name of the character in the play *Speed the Plough* by Thomas Morton.
10. c. Gradgrind. The character who trusts facts and statistics more than emotions in Charles Dickens' *Hard Times*.

11. l. Galahad. The noblest knight of the Round Table in the legend of King Arthur.
12. h. Fagin. The character who trains boys to be pickpockets in Charles Dickens' *Oliver Twist*.

Unit 56

A:
1. antipasto — an appetiser comprising a combination of foods such as smoked meats and grilled vegetables
2. risotto — a rice dish cooked in stock
3. focaccia — a flat bread flavoured with olive oil and topped with herbs
4. vongole — clams
5. gelato — ice cream
6. pesto — a sauce consisting of basil, pine nuts, garlic, olive oil and cheese
7. carbonara — a sauce containing eggs, cheese, and bacon or ham
8. lasagna — a dish made by baking fillings of meat or cheese between layers of flat pasta
9. parmesan — a kind of cheese, usually grated or cut in thin slices and served as a garnish
10. espresso — a strong coffee brewed by forcing steam under pressure through roasted, powdered coffee beans
11. cappuccino — coffee mixed or topped with milk or cream
12. bologna — a seasoned smoked sausage

B:
1. b
2. a
3. a
4. b
5. a
6. b

Unit 57

1. leathery
2. woolly
3. golden
4. rocky
5. rubbery
6. metallic
7. velvety
8. fiery
9. silvery
10. meaty
11. wooden
12. stony
13. glassy
14. waxy
15. flowery
16. watery
17. tinny
18. icy
19. bookish
20. creamy

Unit 58

1. sauntering
2. hobbled
3. shuffle
4. tottered

5. lurched
6. toddling
7. waddled
8. trudged
9. reeling
10. swaggered

11. trek
12. prowl
13. ambled
14. stumbled
15. dawdling

7. spray
8. cascades
9. shimmer

10. glistened
11. ripple
12. radiate

Unit 59

A: 1. fish frying in a pan
2. door opening on a rusty hinge
3. taffeta skirt
4. coins in a pocket
5. jet engine
6. heavy suitcase falling from a height
7. pebble falling into a pond
8. wine cork coming out of a bottle
9. paper burning
10. chair being dragged across a wooden floor
11. whip being brandished
12. booted feet marching
13. refrigerator running
14. wind blowing through stone columns
15. key turning in a lock
16. sudden braking of tyres
17. buttons being shaken in a tin box
18. car engine just before it dies
19. feet walking on soft mud
20. metal dustbin cover falling on cement floor

B: 1. squirt
2. chomped
3. zoom
4. thwacking
5. thumped

6. spurted
7. squashed
8. babble
9. hissed
10. harrumphed

Unit 60

A: **Light:** dazzle, glare, flash, glisten, glow, gleam, shimmer, sparkle, glitter, flicker, glint, beam, illuminate, radiate, scintillate, twinkle

Water/Other Liquids: swirl, ripple, cascade, stream, spray, lap, drip, ooze, trickle, gush, churn, swoosh, swell, rush, seethe, eddy

B: 1. glare
2. trickle
3. lap

4. glow
5. beam
6. flickering

Unit 61

A: **Synonyms for food and drink:** victual, provender, comestibles, viand, vittles, repast, refreshments, cuisine, grub, tuck, chow

Synonyms for chew: masticate, gnaw, nibble, manducate

Words that describe the taste of food: tart, tangy, spicy, bland, piquant, cloying, luscious, juicy, succulent, vinegary, briny, peppery

Words showing methods of preparing and cooking food: saute, fricassee, braise, julienne, blanch, parboil, sear, simmer, brew, broil, percolate, scorch, coddle

Words that describe appetite: voracious, peckish, ravenous, famished

B: 1. nibble; voracious/ ravenous
2. fricassee
3. briny
4. coddle
5. peckish

6. cuisine
7. blanch
8. spicy/piquant; bland
9. refreshments
10. masticates

Unit 62

A: 1. paisley
2. bikini
3. bedlam
4. champagne
5. bohemian

6. denim
7. blarney
8. spartan
9. Coventry
10. canary

B: 1. d
2. h
3. a
4. g

5. b
6. c
7. f
8. e

Unit 63

A:

British English	American English
garden	yard
tap	faucet
pavement	sidewalk
motorway	freeway
biscuit	cookie
lorry	truck
puncture	blow-out
rubbish	garbage
holiday	vacation
queue	line
sweets	candy
wardrobe	closet
taxi	cab
luggage	baggage
autumn	fall
lift	elevator
bill	check
curtains	drapes
pram	baby carriage
nappy	diaper
potato chips	French fries
rubbish bin	trash can
boot	trunk
bonnet	hood

B:
1. The American is more likely to be in a bank. 'Bill' in American English means 'bank note'. If he were in a restaurant, he would ask for the check.
2. You would direct the British visitor to the kitchen as 'wash up' in British English means 'wash the dishes'. If the visitor were American, when she says she wants to wash up, it means she wants to wash her hands, so you would take her to the bathroom.
3. If he were American, you would be handing him his waistcoat. In British English a vest means a sleeveless undergarment. A Brit would call a vest a waistcoat (a sleeveless upper garment that opens down the front and normally has a V-necked opening).
4. You need to climb only one flight of stairs because an American would call the ground floor the first floor.

Unit 64

1. table; tabled
2. dusted; dusted
3. sanctioned; sanctioned
4. handicap; handicap
5. fast; fast
6. trim; trim
7. left; left
8. overlook; overlooked
9. scanned; scanned
10. cleave; cleave
11. tempered; tempered
12. screen; screened

Unit 65

A: Noisy/Loud/Unpleasant
cacophony, clamorous, ear-splitting, strident, hubbub, racket, pandemonium, uproarious, deafening, rambunctious, fortissimo, tumultous, hullabaloo, din, blaring, discordant

Quiet/Soft/Pleasant
hush, muffled, muted, inaudible, pianissimo, stifled, lull, quiescent, sough, murmur, susurration, whisper, dulcet, euphony

B:
1. voluble
2. reticent
3. tight-lipped
4. boisterous
5. uncommunicative
6. laconic
7. stentorian
8. vociferously
9. taciturn
10. fluent

Unit 66

A: Soft/Smooth: sleek, furry, fluffy, feathery, woolly, downy, silky, fleecy, velvety, cottony, satiny, spongy

Hard/Rough/Sharp: bristly, fuzzy, prickly, wiry, stubbly, thorny, gnarled, knotty, knobbly, jagged, serrated, barbed, brambly, spiny, spiky

B:
1. springy
2. flabby
3. doughy
4. squishy
5. brittle
6. sandy
7. mushy
8. gelatinous
9. slippery
10. limp
11. supple
12. elastic
13. pliable
14. pulpy

Unit 67

1. *Illusion* is correct. It means 'false belief'. *Allusion* means 'indirect reference', as in 'This book is full of *allusions* to Greek mythology.'

2. *Biannual* is correct. *Biennial* means 'once in two years'.

3. *Adverse* is correct. It means 'unfavourable' or 'harmful'. *Averse* means 'strongly against' or 'reluctant', as in 'Her father is *averse* to the idea of putting her in a coeducational school as he doesn't trust her with boys.'

4. *Afflicted* is correct. The meanings of the two words are similar but the way they are used is different. Someone is *afflicted* with suffering or trouble but something unpleasant is *inflicted* on a person, as in 'The suffering *inflicted* by the bombing on the people of Hiroshima is indescribable.'

5. *Disinterested* is correct. It means 'impartial' or 'unbiased'. *Uninterested* means 'having no interest', as in 'The teacher was *uninterested* in our excuses and told us to be silent.'

6. *Elicit* is correct. It means 'to call forth' or 'to draw out'. *Illicit* means 'illegal', as in 'He was caught trying to smuggle *illicit* drugs across the border.'

7. *Continual* is correct. It means 'recurring regularly and frequently'. *Continuous* means 'extended without interruption' or 'non-stop', as in 'The siren wailed *continuously* for ten minutes.'

8. *Imminent* is correct. This word is used to describe a situation or event that is about to take place. *Eminent* is used to describe people — and means 'famous' or 'great', as in 'The *eminent* statesman was surrounded by hordes of reporters and photographers.'

9. *Luxurious* is correct. (Unless the condo is so full of growing things that it resembles a jungle!) *Luxurious* means 'expensive' and 'comfortable' while *luxuriant* is used to describe plant growth and means 'growing in abundance' and 'profuse' as in 'The greenhouse is full of *luxuriant* plants imported from all over the world.'

10. *Complement* is correct. It means 'something that completes'. *Compliment* means 'an expression of praise' or 'a flattering remark', as in 'He paid her the ultimate *compliment* of singling her out for the dance.'

11. *Flouting* is correct. It means 'treating with disrespect'. *Flaunting* means 'showing off', as in 'She was shamelessly *flaunting* her new-found wealth by wearing expensive clothes and jewellery to the class reunion.' Rules and regulations are *flouted*. Clothes, cars and other possessions are *flaunted*.

12. *Economic* is correct. You use *economic* when talking about the field of economics. You use *economical* when talking about not being wasteful, as in 'I'm trying to be *economical* by eating at home more often.'

13. *Stationery* is correct. This is the word to use for writing materials. *Stationary* means 'not moving', as in 'The train remained *stationary* for half an hour.'

14. *Principal* is correct. It is used as an adjective here and means 'main' or 'leading'. Of course, you all know what *principal* as a noun means — the head, the most important person in the school! *Principle* is always a noun, and it means 'belief' or 'basic assumption', as in 'Americans believe strongly in the *principles* of democracy.'

15. *Historic* is correct. The words *today* in the sentence rules out the possibility of using *historical*, which is the correct word to use when we talk about events in the past, or about history in general. *Historic* can be used to describe an important, a memorable or a momentous occasion which can take place in the past or present.

16. *Ingenuous* is correct. It means 'naive', 'frank' or 'candid'. *Ingenious* means 'extremely clever' or 'creative', as in 'She came up with an *ingenious* device for extracting water out of the atmosphere.'

17. *Contemptible* is correct. It means 'despicable' or 'deserving contempt'. *Contemptuous*, on the other hand, means 'feeling contempt for' or 'showing scorn', as in 'He is *contemptuous* of anyone born wealthy, as he himself is a self-made millionaire.'

18. *Immoral* is correct. It means 'morally wrong'. *Amoral* means 'not caring about whether something is right or wrong, as in 'The politician's views were completely *amoral*, and led to him losing the support of the conservative community.'

19. *Immigrated* is correct. It means 'entered another country to live'. *Emigrated* means 'left one country to settle in another', as in 'The sisters *emigrated* from Russia.' Remember, 'immigrate *to*' and 'emigrate *from*'.

20. *Forgoing* is correct. It means 'giving up' or 'doing without.' *Foregoing* means 'what went before' or 'preceding', as in 'Pay attention to the *foregoing* instructions in the e-mail.'

Unit 68

A:
1. suspenders
2. compensation
3. pendulous
4. impending
5. dispense
6. expend
7. perpendicular
8. pensive
9. quest
10. inquest
11. inquisitive
12. acquire
13. prerequisite
14. query
15. conquer
16. request

B:
1. prerequisite
2. pendulous
3. conquer
4. compensation
5. quest
6. inquest
7. expend
8. impending
9. acquired
10. request

Unit 69

A:
1. tortuous
2. capacious
3. clamour
4. acclaim
5. extort
6. revolve
7. torture
8. evolution
9. susceptible
10. captivate
11. claim
12. revolt
13. contortionist
14. intercept
15. revolting
16. declaim

Unit 71

A:
1. long crooked branches of an oak tree
2. massive tree trunks growing close together
3. a Persian carpet of autumnal colours
4. sapphire gems
5. a landscape of hills and valleys
6. the sun during the night
7. cotton candy in the sky
8. an impressionistic painting of bold floral whirls and twirls
9. silken threads
10. mosquito coils on the forest ground

B:
1. volcano waiting to erupt
2. mist
3. swimming pool float
4. sunbeam
5. noose around his neck
6. warm sweater on a wintry day
7. fluffy wool ball

8. sinking ship
9. smooth train ride
10. sure-footed mule

C:
1. pricked
2. drowning
3. stole
4. massaged
5. swelled
6. plummeted
7. lighted
8. snuffed
9. sliced
10. dims

D:
1. ocean
2. nightmare
3. harvest
4. loose canon
5. wings
6. blanket
7. crest
8. abyss
9. wall
10. shadow

E:
1. breezy
2. fiery
3. decaffeinated
4. tangled
5. whirling
6. scarred
7. flowery
8. salivating
9. Withering
10. suffocating

Unit 72

A:

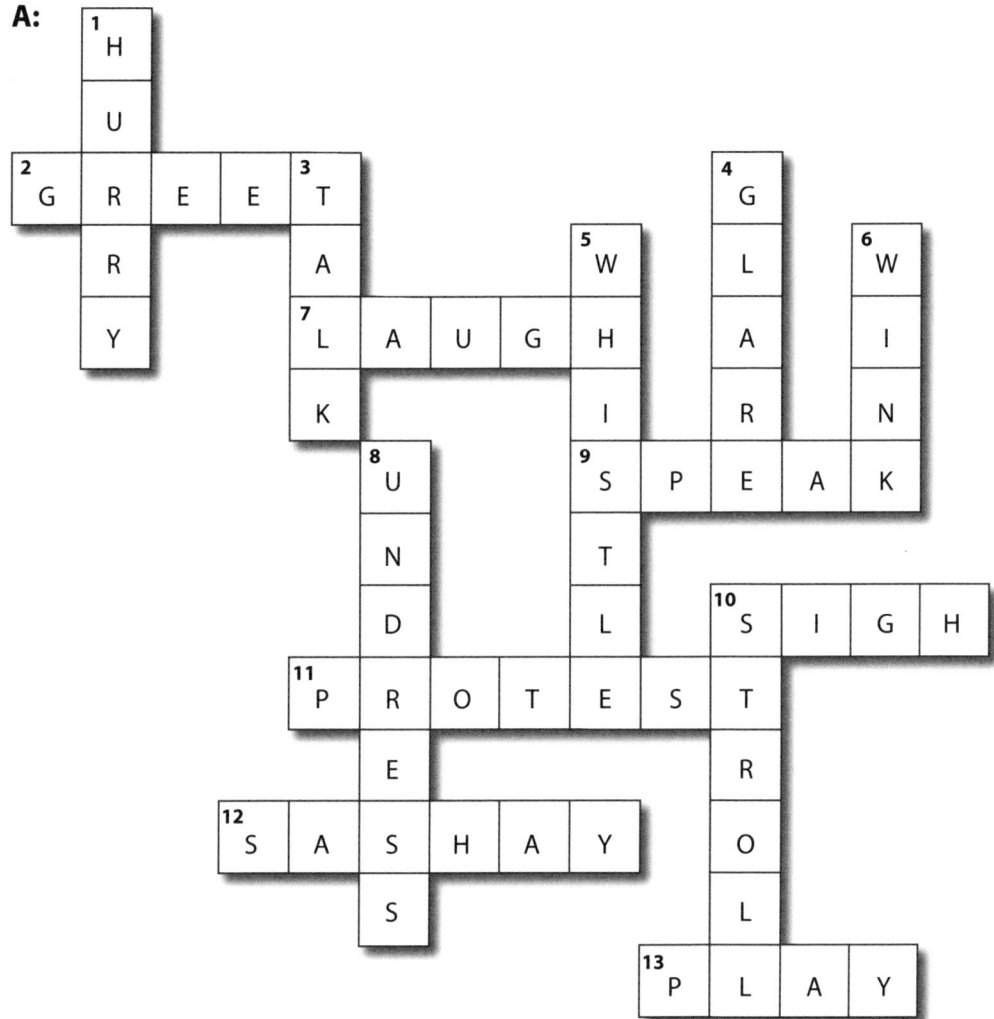

Crossword grid answers:

1 (down) HURRY
2 (across) GREET
3 (down) TAKLK — T A K L K...

7 (across) LAUGH
9 (across) SPEAK
4 (down) GLARE
5 (down) WHINE... WHISTLE
6 (down) WINK
8 (down) UNDS... UNDS
10 (across) SIGH
11 (across) PROTEST
12 (across) SASHAY
13 (across) PLAY

Unit 73

A:
1. insects
2. heredity
3. crop production
4. skin disorders
5. poisons and their treatment
6. word meanings
7. coins
8. injuries of the skeletal system
9. eye diseases
10. nervous system disorders
11. stamps
12. blood disorders

B:
1. plagiarist
2. altruist
3. nonconformist
4. genealogist
5. evangelist
6. therapist
7. naturalist
8. humorist
9. activist
10. pacifist

Unit 74

A:
1. macrophobia — fear of long waits
2. necrophobia — fear of death or dead things
3. cyberphobia — fear of computers
4. felinophobia — fear of cats
5. agoraphobia — fear of open or public places
6. chromophobia — fear of colours
7. claustrophobia — fear of confined spaces
8. kleptophobia — fear of stealing or becoming a thief

B:
1. heights
2. dogs
3. spiders
4. loneliness
5. insects
6. blood
7. water
8. sleep
9. germs
10. dirt
11. snakes
12. disease
13. children
14. ghosts
15. fear
16. light
17. monsters
18. witches
19. strangers
20. animals

C:
1. biophilia — love of nature
2. bibliophilia — love of books
3. anglophilia — love of England and all things English
4. cinephilia — love of movies

Philophobia is the fear of falling in love.

Unit 75

A:
1. g
2. d
3. j
4. h
5. b
6. n
7. a
8. l
9. c
10. i
11. m
12. k
13. f
14. e

B:
1. Biometrics
2. user-friendly
3. road rage
4. angel investor
5. hands-on
6. snail mail
7. makeover
8. sound bites
9. blogs
10. adultescent

Unit 76

1. reformist
2. atheist
3. romanticist
4. altruist
5. hedonist
6. misogynist
7. idealist
8. misogamist
9. masochist
10. sadist
11. misanthropist
12. chauvinist
13. nonconformist
14. optimist
15. pessimist
16. fatalist
17. escapist
18. narcissist
19. nationalist
20. activist
21. pacifist
22. bigamist
23. perfectionist
24. lobbyist
25. exhibitionist
26. pragmatist
27. racist
28. alarmist
29. recidivist
30. socialist
31. anarchist
32. imperialist
33. fundamentalist

Unit 77

1. kohlrabi — a cabbage-like vegetable
2. augment — to increase
3. savannahs — grassy plains
4. evanescent — temporary
5. hectic — very busy
6. vapid — dull, lifeless
7. quintessential — ideal, model
8. saturnine — melancholy
9. euthanasia — killing of a person for merciful reasons
10. covert — secret

Unit 78

1. memorabilia — a collection of things worth remembering
2. paraphernalia — the equipment used in a particular activity
3. precocious — ahead in development, talented
4. bigot — a person who holds extreme views
5. exigency — an occasion which demands urgent attention
6. scrupulous — very careful, meticulous
7. macabre — morbid, ghastly
8. egress — exit, way out
9. lucid — clear, coherent
10. anomaly — deviation from what is normal, oddity

Unit 79

1. nebulous — vague, not clear
2. concur — to agree
3. avarice — extreme greed for money
4. inscrutable — hard to make out
5. turbid — cloudy and dirty
6. ebullient — fun and cheerful
7. diffident — insecure
8. ruminate — to think over carefully
9. rancour — spite and hostility
10. jocular — funny, humorous

Unit 80

1. execrable — terrible, very bad
2. novice — beginner
3. nefarious — evil
4. prolific — producing many works
5. authoritative — highly reliable
6. itinerant — nomadic, travelling from place to place
7. gregarious — outgoing and sociable
8. morose — glum and miserable
9. pristine — not polluted, pure
10. connive — to conspire

Unit 81

1. somnolent — drowsy, sleepy
2. nemesis — an opponent who usually wins
3. crux — major, vital point
4. salutary — healthful, having a good effect on health
5. portend — to forewarn
6. inundated — overwhelmed, weighed down
7. exacerbate — to worsen, to increase in severity
8. remonstrate — to argue in protest, to raise objections
9. aficionado — addict, fan
10. inimical — hostile, unfavourable

Unit 82

1. mien — demeanour, manner
2. abet — to help, to assist
3. bilk — to cheat, to swindle
4. wend — to go forward, to proceed
5. aver — to avow, to state firmly
6. jibe — to taunt, to sneer

7. goad — to incite, to provoke
8. flux — change, fluctuation
9. mire — caught up, involved
10. whit — bit

Unit 83

1. unprecedented — first of its kind, incomparable
2. ultimatum — final deadline before carrying out the threat
3. acrimonious — rancorous, bitter
4. schism — division into opposing factions
5. apprise — to inform
6. esoteric — understood by only a particular group
7. obliterate — to wipe out, to destroy
8. menial — unskilled, tedious
9. oblique — indirect, roundabout
10. putative — alleged, supposed

Unit 84

1. indemnify — to protect against damage
2. litigate — to engage in court proceedings
3. impugn — to attack as false
4. proxy — a person authorised to act for another
5. plaintiff — the person who brings the suit
6. subpoena — to order someone to testify in court
7. prima facie — true or adequate at first sight
8. larceny — theft, the act of taking someone's property unlawfully
9. perjury — lying under oath
10. extradite — to hand over to another government, to send back

Unit 85

1. rubicund — ruddy, indicating health
2. propitious — favourable, promising
3. numinous — spiritual, supernatural
4. sanative — having the power to heal or restore
5. coruscate — to sparkle, to glitter
6. ameliorate — to improve
7. plethoric — excessive in quantity
8. indomitable — resolute, unconquerable
9. blithe — having no worries, carefree
10. paragon — model of perfection, shining example

Unit 86

1. visceral — affecting the body's internal organs
2. unremitting — chronic, constant
3. analgesic — pain-relieving, anti-pain
4. advent — arrival, beginning
5. subjective — personal, individual
6. malinger — to feign illness to avoid work
7. redeeming — good, compensating for some fault
8. alert — to warn, to notify
9. exacerbate — to worsen, to aggravate
10. abominable — terrible, dreadful

Unit 87

1. inexorable — relentless, inescapable
2. adamantine — unyielding, steadfast
3. puissant — strong, powerful
4. Sisyphean — futile and needing a lot of effort
5. sepulchral — deathly, sombre
6. onerous — wearisome, troublesome
7. squalid — poor and dirty
8. obdurate — stubborn, hardhearted
9. beleaguer — to beset with difficulties, to harass
10. diabolical — cruel, evil

Unit 88

1. zaftig — full-figured, plump
2. zany — crazy
3. zap — to destroy
4. zealot — a fervent supporter of a cause
5. zeitgeist — the spirit of the time
6. zenith — the highest point attained
7. zephyr — a gentle breeze
8. zilch — nothing
9. zing — energy, vigour
10. zonked — exhausted, extremely tired

Unit 89

1. diatribe — a critical speech
2. ebullition — a sudden outburst of emotion
3. rodomontade — a bragging speech
4. dulcet — pleasant, melodious
5. obtund — to dull, to deaden
6. cacophony — a jarring, discordant sound
7. kvetch — to complain in a whining way

8. vociferous — noisy, determined (in a loud way)
9. mollify — to calm down, to pacify
10. stentorian — extremely loud

Unit 90

1. savoir-faire — social competence
2. outré — bizarre
3. c'est la vie — that's life
4. déjà vu — the feeling that you have seen or experienced what you are feeling now
5. avant-garde — modern, unusually innovative
6. insouciance — a cheerful feeling without worry or guilt
7. pique — to annoy, to irritate
8. ennui — boredom
9. echelon — level, rank
10. précis — concise summary
11. laissez-faire — unwillingness to get involved

Unit 91

1. incognito — in disguise, anonymously
2. imbroglio — a complicated heated argument
3. a poco a poco — little by little
4. cognoscenti — experts in a field, especially the arts
5. sotto voce — very softly
6. salvo — sudden outburst of cheers or praise
7. vertu — love of arts and fine things
8. prima donna — someone who demands a lot of attention
9. virtuoso — extremely skilled
10. a cappella — without any musical instruments

Unit 92

1. ad nauseam — to a nauseating or sickening extent
2. status quo — the existing state or condition
3. bona fide — authentic, genuine
4. persona non grata — unwelcome person
5. alter ego — other self, someone most like you in disposition
6. non sequitur — an irrelevant or unrelated reply
7. quid pro quo — a fair exchange
8. in extremis — at the moment of death
9. vice versa — the other way round

10. magnum opus — masterpiece, the most important work by a writer
11. deus ex machina — very unlikely end to a story
12. ad hoc — not regular or planned

Unit 93

1. desultory — irregular, occurring randomly
2. specious — deceptively attractive or pleasing, false
3. ominous — unpromising, threatening
4. aberrant — uncharacteristic, abnormal
5. peremptory — urgent, authoritative, commanding
6. stupendous — astounding, amazing
7. nonchalant — indifferent, casual
8. dolorous — cheerless, miserable
9. prodigious — enormous, extremely large
10. vehement — full of emotion, passionate

Unit 94

1. sporadically — irregularly, now and then
2. superfluously — unnecessarily
3. poignantly — emotionally, sentimentally
4. parsimoniously — frugally, thriftily
5. perfunctorily — showing little interest
6. spuriously — incorrectly, falsely
7. surreptitiously — secretly, sneakily
8. ruefully — sorrowfully, regretfully
9. relentlessly — persistently, unyieldingly
10. voraciously — avidly, in an extremely eager manner

Unit 95

1. polyglot — a multilingual person
2. stigma — a mark of shame or disgrace
3. candour — honesty, openness
4. compunction — reluctance, regret
5. ebullience — enthusiasm, exuberance
6. hiatus — break, interval
7. paucity — scarcity, small number
8. proclivity — inclination, tendency
9. umbrage — offence, resentment
10. contrition — remorse, regret

Unit 96

1. tarnish — to damage, to harm
2. reprieve — to cancel punishment (especially by hanging)
3. placate — to pacify, to calm down
4. manifest — to demonstrate, to show
5. manoeuvre — to act cunningly to achieve a goal, to scheme
6. vacillate — to waver, to dither
7. vindicate — to free from blame, to pardon
8. stultify — to render useless or ineffectual, to cripple
9. enthuse — to express with enthusiasm
10. aggrandise — to improve, to enhance

Unit 97

1. assail
   a. to worry or upset
   b. to criticise, to berate

2. chafe
   a. to rub and cause irritation
   b. to annoy

3. detect
   a. to discover, to find
   b. to perceive, to sense

4. remote
   a. slight, faint
   b. isolated, secluded, out-of-the-way

5. verge
   a. to come close to
   b. to be on the edge/border

6. trace
   a. to follow the trail of
   b. sign of evidence

7. embellishment
   a. decoration, adornment
   b. untrue/fabricated detail

8. infernal
   a. showing anger or fury
   b. resembling or characteristic of hell

9. primitive
    a. uncomfortable and not modern
    b. ancient, very old

10. culminate
    a. to come to completion, to end
    b. to reach the highest point of development, to climax

Unit 98

1. contemplate
    a. to think about very carefully, to ponder
    b. to have in mind as a possibility

2. plausible
    a. credible, believable
    b. smooth-tongued with deceptive intentions

3. decline
    a. to weaken, to fail, to deteriorate
    b. to refuse, to reject

4. penetrate
    a. to enter and gain a market share
    b. to understand, to succeed in understanding something

5. desolate
    a. deserted, uninhabited
    b. depressing, gloomy

6. shroud
    a. to cover
    b. burial garment

7. rival
    a. competitor, opponent
    b. to match, to equal

8. flourish
    a. to grow well
    b. to wave something in your hand

9. significant
    a. major, important
    b. considerable, substantial

10. fashion
    a. trend, style
    b. to make into something, to shape, to mould

Unit 99

1. holding fast onto something, firm
2. speech where the actor speaks to himself, monologue
3. feeding on grass
4. being in love, indicating love or sexual desire
5. to speak evil of, to make harmful statements
6. material assets
7. resulting from mental or emotional causes
8. being unfaithful
9. shaped like a star, radiating from the centre
10. relating to the physical world, relating to the body, of a material nature

Unit 100

1. conflicting, uncertain, undecided
2. to work from home via the computer network
3. to occur before
4. hindering the achievement of a goal, achieving the opposite result
5. outside the range of the five senses
6. looking back
7. relating to the earth's internal heat
8. figurative expression employing exaggeration
9. newcomer to a field, new participant in an activity
10. supposedly scientific but not supported by evidence

Unit 101

1. (adjective) capable of grasping
2. (noun) audacity, nerve
3. (verb) to do something with little preparation
4. (adjective) dour, morose, sullen
5. (adjective) childish, infantile
6. (adjective) mysterious, mystifying, enigmatic
7. (noun) eye defect causing distorted/blurred images
8. (adverb) strongly, forcefully, fiercely
9. (noun) final outcome, climax
10. (verb) instruct, enlighten
11. (noun) predicament, difficult situation

12. (adjective) showing sound judgement, wise, judicious
13. (noun) natural inclination, tendency, disposition
14. (adjective) astute, perceptive, shrewd
15. (adjective) persistent in wrongdoing, unyielding, stubborn
16. (verb) make unnecessary
17. (adjective) related to learning by enquiry and investigation
18. (adjective) easily felt, tangible
19. (noun) spirit of the times, cultural or moral climate of an era
20. (adjective) indifferent, careless, unenthusiastic

Unit 102

1.	c	11.	r
2.	k	12.	n
3.	j	13.	o
4.	a	14.	e
5.	t	15.	q
6.	p	16.	l
7.	g	17.	i
8.	s	18.	m
9.	h	19.	d
10.	b	20.	f

Unit 103

1.	j	11.	o
2.	p	12.	b
3.	g	13.	n
4.	h	14.	r
5.	c	15.	d
6.	t	16.	s
7.	i	17.	k
8.	f	18.	e
9.	q	19.	m
10.	a	20.	l

GCE 'O' Level Words You Should Know (Also Answers To Part 3)

A:
abandon	leave behind
abashed	ashamed
abhor	hate
abscond	make off
abundance	large quantity
accede	consent
accelerate	step up
accumulate	build up
acute	serious
adamant	resolute
adroit	skilful
advance	move forwards
affluent	wealthy
alleviate	lessen
alter	change
ameliorate	improve
angle	point of view
annual	yearly
anomaly	abnormality
antipathy	ill will
aplomb	self-confidence
apparent	evident
appreciate	increase in value
apt	appropriate
arid	dry
arrogant	conceited
assail	attack
astounding	amazing
attain	accomplish
attract	appeal to
augment	add to
awry	wrong

B:
baffle	confuse
banished	exiled
banter	tease
barely	only just
baulk	refuse to do something
bear	tolerate
beguile	captivate
belligerent	aggressive
belt	band

bereft	completely without hope
besotted	smitten
boon	advantage
brandish	wave
bravado	boldness
breach	violation
bridle	restrain
broach	bring up
brusque	curt

C:
carnivorous	meat-eating
censure	criticise
chafe	scrape
chief	most important
clearly	without a doubt
compliant	conforming
concentration	attentiveness
concur	agree
conscious	aware
consequently	as a result
constantly	all the time
contemplate	think about
convey	express
cover	protection
credit	acclaim
crucial	necessary
culminate	end
currently	at this time
curtail	cut back

D:
debility	weakness
decline	deteriorate
deduce	infer
defunct	out of use
demonstrate	show
dense	thick
depict	represent
deserted	solitary
desolate	gloomy
detached	aloof
detect	spot
deviation	departure

	devise	work out	
	dictate	order	
	dilapidated	rundown	
	diminish	shrink	
	direction	course	
	disparate	contrasting	
	diverse	different	
	dogged	steadfast	
	dominate	overshadow	

E:

efface	wipe out
effectively	successfully
egregious	conspicuously bad
emancipate	set free
embellishment	decoration
emerge	appear
eminent	well-known
enticing	alluring
entire	whole
epitome	typical example
equitable	fair
escape	flight
eventually	sooner or later
evidence	confirmation
exaggerated	blown up
expected	usual
expedient	useful
expiate	compensate
extend	enlarge
extricate	disentangle

F:

fade	lighten
fashion	shape
ferment	confusion
figment	imagined thing
finicky	particular
fitfully	restlessly
flaccid	limp
flagrant	open
flee	escape
flourish	thrive
foment	provoke
force	power
fortuitous	unexpected
fragments	wreckage
frequent	habitual
fresh	clean
futile	vain

G:

galvanise	stir up
gauge	estimate
genial	friendly
genuinely	indisputably
gnarled	contorted
gradually	steadily
grasp	seize
gratuitous	free
grave	solemn
groundwork	foundation
gyrate	rotate

H:

hazardous	dangerous
heinous	terrible
hiatus	break
hinder	obstruct
hoard	put aside
homage	respect
hover	linger
humid	moist

I:

image	picture
imminent	about to happen
impact	influence
inedible	unpalatable
inevitable	unstoppable
infallible	perfect
infernal	awful
inherent	natural
initially	at first
instance	case in point
instantly	right away
intelligible	understandable
interminable	endless
interrupt	intrude
intimidate	threaten
inundate	overwhelm
invaluable	priceless
inveigh	protest vehemently
itinerant	roaming

J:

jaded	tired
jaunty	lively
jeer	laugh at
jeopardise	put at risk
jilt	split up with
jocular	funny
jubilant	thrilled

judicious	wise	moderate	reasonable
junction	intersection	monotonous	dull
juncture	point in time	mundane	routine
jurisdiction	authority	myriad	countless
justified	acceptable	mystified	bewildered
juvenile	young		
juxtapose	put next to	**N:** negligent	careless

K: kaleidoscope	series of changing phases	negligible	insignificant
		nicety	small point
keen	sharp	nimble	agile
kickstart	set in motion	nondescript	ordinary
kindle	incite	notion	idea
kinship	relationship	notorious	infamous
knell	signal of disaster	nourish	nurture
knoll	hill	nuance	tone
knowingly	with intent	nuisance	irritation
kudos	reputation	nullify	cancel out
kvetch	complain persistently		

O: objective — unprejudiced

L: lavish	plentiful	obsolescent	falling into disuse
leach	trickle	obsolete	no longer in use
lead	direct	obtrusive	unmistakable
level	flat	obviate	prevent
levity	light-heartedness	obvious	clear
liability	responsibility	offend	insult
libel	defame	offer	suggest
likely	prone	ominous	boding evil
lithe	agile	opportune	appropriate
livid	enraged	overdue	behind time
lucid	clear	overwhelming	tremendous
ludicrous	absurd		
lugubrious	mournful	**P:** particularly	exceptionally
luxuriant	fertile	penetrating	insightful
		perfunctory	unthinking

M: main	key	peripheral	minor
mandatory	compulsory	permanent	lasting
manifest	show	persecute	discriminate against
mask	disguise	persona	assumed role
maximum	utmost	perspective	viewpoint
mediocre	average	pertinent	relevant
menial	tedious	phenomenal	extraordinary
mercurial	volatile	phenomenon	observable fact
merely	simply	pioneer	lead the way
milieu	environment	pivotal	crucial
mobile	movable	plausible	credible
model	reproduction	plethora	excess
		pocket	steal
		populous	densely inhabited

precious	valuable
predicament	dilemma
prerequisite	requirement
previous	earlier
primarily	chiefly
primordial	primitive
princely	substantial
principal	major
principle	code
pristine	unspoilt
promise	pledge
prosecute	put on trial
provoke	inflame
punitive	corrective

Q:
quash	defeat
querulous	irritable
quiescent	quiet
quintessence	perfect example

R:
range	variety
readily	promptly
recede	move away
recoup	get back
refurbish	restore
regularly	habitually
reign	time in power
relic	historical object
remote	distant
reputation	standing
resilient	flexible
respite	relief
retrieve	take back
rich	loaded
rigour	harshness
rival	adversary

S:
sanction	permission
scarcely	only just
secret	undisclosed
seep	leak
senseless	ridiculous
shear	shave
shed	discard
sheer	steep
shroud	cover
significant	important
signify	indicate

slacken	relax
slender	lean
spectator	viewer
spur	encourage
squander	waste
staunch	faithful
stealthily	silently
stigma	shame
stipulate	specify
strident	loud
stringent	rigorous
sublime	inspiring
sufficient	ample
support	hold up
surreptitious	secret
sustain	keep up
systematically	methodically

T:
tacit	unspoken
tamper	interfere
tardy	sluggish
tedious	dreary
tend	look after
titillate	thrill
torpid	lazy
torrent	gush
torrid	hot
tortuous	complex
torturous	agonising
total	complete
trace	sign
traverse	pass through
trigger	set off
triumphant	victorious
turn	curve

U:
ulterior	hidden
unanimous	undivided
uncompromising	rigid
unconscionable	unscrupulous
underlying	primary
ungainly	awkward
universal	worldwide
unobtrusive	modest
unprecedented	first-time
unrequited	unreturned
untimely	premature
unwary	unsuspecting

upheaval	disturbance	
urge	exhort	
utilise	make use of	

V:

vacuous	blank
vagrant	wandering
valiant	heroic
veneer	surface
verge	border
verify	prove
verve	energy
vestige	trace
vicarious	shocking
vicinity	neighbourhood
vicissitudes	difficulties
vigilant	watchful
voracious	greedy
vulnerable	defenceless

W:

wacky	mad
waif	soul
waive	give up
watershed	turning point
weld	connect
wheedle	persuade

whine	complain
wholesome	nourishing
will	resolve
wilt	droop
wily	crafty
wisp	fragment
wit	humour
withstand	endure
wondrous	amazing
wound	hurt
wrath	anger

Y:

yank	pull
yarn	tall story
yield	produce

Z:

zany	crazy
zealous	keen
zenith	peak
zest	appetite